AF345342

candles on the path

Candles on the Path

Excerpts from the teachings of
Shaykh Mohamed Faouzi al-Karkari

Translated by **Marouen Jedoui**

LES 7 LECTURES

Candles on the Path is published by the nonprofit organization
Anwar and his publishing house Les 7 Lectures

44 Fernand Brunfaut Street
1080 Brussels, Belgium

© Les 7 Lectures, 2024
All rights reserved

ISBN: 978-2-930978-92-5
Deposit number: D/2024/14.291/03 (Belgium)
Legal Deposit: february 2024

All rights reserved. No part of this publication may be reproduced,
distributed, or transmitted in any form or by any means, including
photocopying, recording, or other electronic or mechanical
methods, without the prior written permission of the publisher,
except in the case of brief quotations embodied in critical
reviews and certain other non commercial uses permitted by
copyright law. For permission requests, write to the publisher

أعوذ بالله من الشيطان الرجيم

بسم الله الرحمن الرحيم

بسم الله الرحمن الرحيم

بسم الله الرحمن الرحيم

بسم الله

بسم الله

بسم الله

الله

الله

الله

ولا حول ولا قوة إلا بالله العلي العظيم

Table of Contents

Preface

In the unfolding journey of spiritual awakening, aspirants navigate routes frequently mingled with moments of uncertainty, revelation, and deep reflection. Regrettably, books that delve into complex concepts sometimes fail to address the fundamental questions and dilemmas novice disciples encounter at the outset of their spiritual quest. This is why our Shaykh, Sidi Mohamed Faouzi al-Karkari (*Quddisa Sirruh*), advises newcomers to the path to concentrate solely on two seminal works: "The Foundations" (*al-kawākib an-nūrāniyya*) and "The Sufi Path of Light" (*al-maḥajja al-baydhā'*), refraining from perusing his more advanced texts.

Observing the growing curiosity and eagerness of English-speaking disciples—who sometimes find it unsatisfactory to rely solely on these two foundational volumes—I felt compelled to translate select portions of the Shaykh's lectures into a collection that would benefit both advanced and less experienced disciples.

Regrettably, the Shaykh's *durūs* are not automatically translated for English-speaking disciples. This is unfortunate, as they are a crucial source of guidance and reflection. Furthermore, they have not been made available in written English, which would be a valuable resource for all who are interested. Within these sessions, disciples find answers and insights into their inner dilemmas and concerns, often through subtle hints from the Shaykh. Moreover, these gatherings provide a platform where disciples can gauge their progression on the path, interpreting the Shaykh's indirect guidance to navigate their spiritual journey.

Embarking on this translation venture, I realized that the Shaykh's lectures might be too intricate and potentially bewildering for newcomers if presented in their entirety, owing to their dense content and the immersive live interaction they entail. Consequently, I chose to encapsulate the essence of these sessions in succinct yet powerful snippets that encapsulate themes I deemed vital for newcomers to acquaint themselves with. This approach is designed to facilitate a more focused and comprehensible way of understanding the complex teachings presented. In doing so, I took great care to maintain the unique discursive style that is characteristic of the Shaykh. I, indeed, firmly believe that it is vital for English-speaking disciples to deeply immerse themselves in the rich and profound methods of discourse that Sidi Shaykh utilizes in his teachings.

Navigating the Shaykh's unique teaching style, characterized by its "patchwork-like" approach to addressing a range of subjects, can be quite challenging. This method, distinguished by its intricate depth, is familiar to Arabic-speaking disciples who have gradually adapted to it over time. I earnestly hope that this work will not only bridge the gap between the English-speaking disciples and the rest of the Karkaris but also provide a rich terrain for exploration, deepening all readers' understanding of their spiritual journeys. Moreover, this initiative aims to enhance the spiritual connection between disciples and their Shaykh. By offering a written platform for English-speaking wayfarers, it seeks to deepen their engagement with the Shaykh's profound teachings, fostering their love for Sidi Shaykh and deepening their appreciation for the Karkariya spiritual path.

It is important to emphasize that most excerpts in this book were recorded just before or after the descent of the reading of *lām al-ʿishq*. This timing renders the book especially pertinent to the current stage of the tariqa. Drafted in mid-2023, it aligns with the time when Karkaris are deeply engaged in studying this exhalted letter of the Supreme Divine Name. The content equips disciples with essential knowledge for navigating the present stage of the Tariqa. While these excerpts cover a broad spectrum of themes, they collectively present the foundational principles of *sulūk* (wayfaring) and spiritual knowledge (*maʿrifa*) vital for understanding and engaging with Sidi Shaykh. I reiterate my hope that this work will aid English-speaking newcomers in catching up with their fellow disciples. Indeed, this book proves invaluable when read early on in the journey. I'm confident that it will accelerate the progress for newcomers, saving them time and effort on the path.

In the summer of 2023, I initiated this translation project, completing it within the same season. The process was significantly less daunting than I had initially anticipated, largely due to the spiritual assistance of Sidi Shaykh (*Quddisa Sirruh*). However, I must acknowledge that the primary challenge of this project was logistical.

I was based at the *Zāwiya* in Morocco, a setting where the conveniences I am accustomed to—such as consistent access to a computer and the freedom to dictate my daily schedule—were not readily available. Consequently, I found myself seizing moments here and there to advance the project, largely relying on my phone and a particularly handy app to gather the translations. It is still remarkable to think that I managed to draft the initial version within just a couple of weeks at the *Zāwiya*, a feat that undeniably attests to our Shaykh's spiritual influence and guidance, rather than the efforts of my mere darkened self.

During this period, I successfully compiled over 40 significant excerpts and translated them into English. Notably, a considerable amount of the necessary material was readily available on the disciples' Facebook pages. I would like to express my sincere appreciation to Sidi Suhayl (Adrien) for generously offering a wealth of material he had translated into French on his Facebook profile. His efforts have substantially enriched the content of this book, with almost half the material consisting of English adaptations of his French translations.

I am equally indebted to Sidi Jamal Ouyang and Sidi Moeen Ahmad, who assisted in transcribing three pivotal responses to English-speaking disciples during our time at the *Zāwiya* in al-Aroui that summer. Their efforts have been instrumental in shaping this project. Moreover, I cannot overlook the unwavering support extended by my family throughout this endeavor. Their encouragement and assistance have been the linchpin in bringing this project to fruition; without them, it simply wouldn't have materialized.

Lastly, I extend my deepest gratitude to Sidi Shaykh Mohamed Faouzi al-Karkari for granting me the opportunity to embark on this project. I am honored to serve as a modest vessel through which his illuminating teachings can reach audiences in the United States and other English-speaking regions.

With humble efforts and a hopeful heart,

Marouen Jedoui
Yale University, New Haven

1.
Luminous *Adab*

The Shaykh of our *shuyūkh*, Sidi Mūlay al-`Arbi al-Darqāwī (*Quddisa Sirruh*), said: "If the *ādāb* (sg. *adab*) are observed, the journey will be fulfilled. Without *ādāb*, there will be neither propriety nor journey."

The true spiritual journey leading the disciple along the paths of spiritual ascension towards the divine presence cannot be realized without complete adherence to the conventions of propriety (*adab*) established over centuries by Sufi masters and inheritors of the Muhammadan Light. Access to the presence of the Real (*Al-Ḥaqq*) requires educating one's body and heart in absolute servitude, akin to a "slave" entering a king's court.

To apply these rules with the Creator, they must first be practiced with the Prophet ﷺ. And to use them with the Prophet ﷺ, they must be applied with one's brethren on the Path and with the realized Shaykh, a deputy (*Walī*) of Allah ﷻ. In this context, understanding and applying the rules of *adab* is fundamental for the seeker of Allah ﷻ (*murīd*) to elevate spiritually in the luminous presence of the Truth. Hence, the companionship of a true, accomplished, and realized Shaykh is imperative.

Shaykh Abu Yazid al-Bistāmī (*Quddisa Sirruh*) stated in this regard that "He who has no Shaykh, *Shaytān* is his Shaykh." Without a guide, one finds himself trapped in the illusory darkness of his ego with no prospect of escape, making him susceptible to the misguidance of *Shaytān*. Others have remarked, "Without the educating Shaykh (*shaykh at-tarbiya*), I would not have known my Lord," signifying that entry into the circle of divine presence (*al-ḥaḍra al-aqdasiyya*) and spiritual knowledge (*ma`rifa*) can't be realized without the guidance of a realized Shaykh. Such a Shaykh must be among the elite of the Prophetic progeny and an inheritor of the Prophet's ﷺ Light, aligning with Jabir's ؓ statement: "I am the City of Knowledge, and `Ali is its gate." To enter the City, one must pass through the gate.

2.
How to Discern the Authentic Shaykh?

Indeed, blessed by the divine grace of the path I have undertaken, I find that many eager souls, immersed in their spiritual journey, often come forward with an earnest query that touches upon the core of the Tariqa. They ask, "How can I be certain that the Shaykh I am following is the true Shaykh, my Shaykh, and what is the ultimate aspiration within the Tariqa? What is it that I strive towards?"

To truly understand the essence of the Shaykh and to discern the authenticity of his spiritual station, one needs to revert to the profound teachings laid out in the Holy Quran and the cherished practices of the Sunna. You see, the Quran, the divine word of Allah ﷻ, proclaims that Allah ﷻ stands as the *Walī*, the protector and guide of those who hold firm in their belief. Thus, it is through a profound sense of belief, an unwavering *Īmān*, that one finds the recognition of the *Walī*. As the Quran explains, the *Walī*, who embodies this divine Name, is someone who has been chosen to guide others from the encompassing darkness towards the witnessing and the realization of the divine Light[1]. Therefore, the true tes-

....

1   Sūra 2. Al-Baqarah, verse 257.

tament of a Shaykh lies in the Light that he embodies and imparts.

Now, you must understand that there exists a variety of avenues to recognize and authenticate the spiritual stature of a Shaykh. The foremost method, particularly for those blessed with innate insight, transcends the need for direct signs. They discern the truth through the experiences and testimonies of others, observing the lives transformed and enlightened through the Tariqa, bearing witness to the divine Light that tens of thousands have already testified to seeing and benefiting immensely from the guidance of the Shaykh.

Consider this, how is it possible for so many individuals to walk upon this righteous path, witnessing awakened divine visions and making consistent spiritual progress, and yet be in error? It presents a profound contradiction to argue against the authenticity of a Shaykh while the Light of God manifests so vividly, serving as an unmistakable guide and companion for all of the *mu'mins*.

In this journey, you might also encounter individuals who, despite having experienced the transformative *bay`a* and witnessed the divine Light, still harbor doubts and succumb to the whispers of the *Shaytān* and to the *waswasa* of the *nafs*. It is during such moments that they must introspect, realizing that perhaps the inadequacy lies within themselves, a turmoil stirred by unfounded doubts.

Know, O disciples, that there exists a blessed faction who, having undertaken the *bay`a*, have beheld the splendid Light of God. These individuals occupy a distinctive place of spiritual realization, having validated the Shaykh's divine linkage. There is no space left for them to spiral into doubts; they resonate with personal experiences and the affirmations of others, witnessing the miracles, the *karāma*, granted to the *Walī* by Allah ﷻ.

It is incumbent upon a *Walī*, who has inherited the blessed path of our Prophet ﷺ, to unveil to his disciples the resplendent verses of the Quran. Just as our Prophet ﷺ, an "illiterate" yet divinely guided messenger, was graced with the comprehensive words of God (*jawāmiʿ al-kalim*), a *Walī* must manifest, at the very least, the radiant verse of Light for his disciples. This verse crystallizes into their hearts the fourfold exemplification of the divine light, serving as a luminous beacon guiding them on their sacred journey towards the pinnacle of enlightenment and a deeper closeness with Allah ﷻ.

In response to the secondary inquiry concerning the disciple's objectives and aspirations within the Tariqa, I will explain the essence of your journey within this sacred path.

O aspirant in pursuit of divine knowledge, your footsteps in the path should be firmly grounded with an unwavering intent to know Allah ﷻ, to immerse in the illuminating recognition of His Divine Light. This pursuit transcends mere intellectual acknowledgment, beckoning you to foster a spiritual cognizance that resonates deeply within your very essence.

Your solemn duty as a disciple, a seeker in this revered path, is to attain *Maʿrifa* - the realized spiritual knowledge of the Divine. This sacred knowledge unveils itself as you venture into the profound realms of self-exploration and realization. Through the contemplative journey within your inner self, you are granted the divine opportunity to discern the intricacies of your own existence, thereby accessing a more profound communion with the Almighty. In this sanctified journey, you will discern moments where your own *nafs* may falter, straying from the righteous path. It becomes your holy obligation, a testament to your growth in Tariqa, to cultivate awareness of these deviations. It is your sacred duty to mend and purify your *nafs*, to align it with the luminous path that leads towards divine closeness.

As you engage in this process of nurturing and refining your *nafs*, be ever vigilant, for heightened awareness fosters a sublime transformation within, guiding you closer to the illuminated soul depicted in the Quranic verse: **"O tranquil soul! Return to your Lord, well pleased and well pleasing. So join My servants, and enter my Paradise."**[2]

....

2   Sūra 89. Al-Fajr, verse 27-30.

3.
Navigating Uncertainty:
Spiritual Authorization and Doubt

A doubtful disciple mentioned meeting someone in a Moroccan city who told him about another branch of the Tariqa Karkariya, originating from our Shaykh Al-Hajj al-Hassan (*Quddisa Sirruh*). He asked how to confirm if this branch is the legitimate one and whether it is necessary to ascertain that I am a genuine successor of the Prophet ﷺ and has proper authorization.

Indeed, my disciples, verifying the authenticity of a spiritual path, such as the Tariqa Karkariya, is a crucial matter. Let me begin by emphasizing that the claim of inheriting the spiritual legacy of our beloved Shaykh should not be taken lightly. This is a profound responsibility!

The individual claiming to be the inheritor of my Shaykh is actually my Shaykh's son. He professes to be a Shaykh, a *Walī*, endowed with the authority to guide people in their spiritual journey towards Allah ﷻ. However, to discern the true inheritors of this spiritual lineage, one must gaze deeply into the manifestations borne within their disciples. For as the ancients in the realm of Sufism have imparted, the true measure of a Shaykh is reflected in the transformations ignited within the hearts of his followers. The sacred energy, the *himma*, that the Shaykh embodies, inevitably blossoms within those who sit at his feet, absorbing the spiritual nourishments he imparts.

Now, travel far and wide, and you will encounter many who claim to be guides on this path. As a disciple, it is your duty to challenge these claims with the Quranic directive, **"Provide your proof if you are truthful."**[3] Therefore, I encourage you, who have been swayed by these uncertainties, to explore that other branch and perhaps other Tariqas, especially since you have not undergone spiritual seclusion (*khulwa*) yet. Some of my followers have faced the same doubts you are grappling with now and chose to explore that other branch, distancing themselves from me. Some remained there for months, others for years, yet the majority came back, while others eventually abandoned them, recognizing a fundamental deficiency.

Please, understand that spiritual permission (*idhn*) from one Shaykh to another isn't a mere formality on paper. It's the transmission of divine light, the unveiling of sacred secrets, and the true tangible guidance toward a complete annihilation in Allah ﷻ. Look around you here, in this Karkariya *Zāwiya*, and you'll find numerous written accreditations from esteemed Shaykhs across the world. But I stress that these papers are inconsequential; they are but shadows of the true spiritual permission.

....

3   Sūra 2. Al-Baqarah, verse 111

Again, it is your right and duty, disciples, to verify your spiritual path, for the Prophet Muhammad ﷺ advised us to choose our guides wisely. Seek what you truly desire and wherever you find it, stay and follow those who can nurture your soul.

Now, allow me to shed light on the lineage of my Shaykh. He is my uncle, the older brother of my father, which means they share the same father. Why would my father, who is deeply committed to the spiritual path, pledge allegiance to me if I was a deceitful pretender? Know that Mūlay Tayeb, my father, not only took *bay`a* with me but also performed the spiritual seclusion (*khulwa*) under our supervision, where he experienced divine openings that led him to dedicate his home as a *Zāwiya*. This profound commitment and recognition of his son's spiritual authority should dispel any doubts.

Consider also this perspective: my father possesses a majestic and commanding personality, a true *jabarūtī* one. Why would he have humbled himself by wearing the *subḥa* and patched cloak (*muraqqa`a*) unless he had a genuine calling? He also supports the Tariqa financially and facilitates the spread of its message. Why would he support his son's claim if there were no truth to it? Why wouldn't he claim to be a Shaykh himself? After all he was the closest person to his father and his older brother, Mūlay Taher and Mūlay al-Hassan.

Now, ponder this, heedless disciple. Think of your own family. Could you convince your mother to follow you as her spiritual guide? Yet, my family and I testify that I am a *Walī*, and they have followed me as their spiritual guide. Find me even one person who would claim that the leader of the other branch is a *Walī*, and I will grant you the honor of becoming a Shaykh in my *Zāwiya*.

I want you to understand that I do not need to resort to false claims or fabricated documents like some others might. My advice to you, my disciple, is to temporarily set aside your patched cloak (*muraqqaʿa*) and *subḥa* and immerse yourself in the other branches, whether of this Tariqa or others, for a period of time. Absorb their teachings, their experiences, and their *waswasa*, and when you return, share your insights!

Now, let's explore this matter from the perspective of the Prophetic hadiths. He prophesied that every century would witness a *mujaddid*, a reviver of faith. Consider this timeline: Shaykh Al-Alawi (*Quddisa Sirruh*) was born in 1874, and I was born in 1974. He founded his *Zāwiya* in 1914, and I established mine in 2014. Let's also delve into the history of the Tariqa's name, Karkariya. Before my era, people did not refer to it as the Tariqa Karkariya; it was known as the Tariqa Alawiya. During the era of my Shaykh, Hajj Al-Hasan (*Quddisa Sirruh*), it bore the name Tariqa Alawiya, not Tariqa Karkariya. He had four disciples, and the last one to undergo spiritual seclusion (*Khulwa*) was his son, who now claims the mantle of Shaykh. Before him, Mūlay Taher, his father, had numerous disciples. All these individuals, including his son, were followers of the Tariqa Alawiya, not Karkariya. Mūlay Taher, our Shaykh's predecessor and our grandfather, initiated many into the practice of spiritual seclusion (*Khulwa*) within the Tariqa Alawiya, fostering the growth of many Sufi

Shuyūkh. Despite receiving spiritual guidance from Mūlay Taher, they identified not as Karkari, but as Alawi.

The term Tariqa Karkariya, as you know it today, came into being during my time. I am the one who introduced this name to the world, building its foundational principles, authoring its books, and nurturing disciples both spiritually and academically. Unlike the earlier generations of Alawiya followers who adhered to the teachings of Shaykh Ahmed Al-Alawi (*Quddisa Sirruh*), our Tariqa is marked by the study of my light, my books, and my spiritual guidance. Our disciples are not ordinary; they encompass doctors, PhD holders, and individuals with exceptional academic backgrounds. If you consider yourself a person of knowledge or spirituality, you will find enlightenment within our ranks.

As you can see the Tariqa has expanded globally and no longer requires external accreditation. In the past, such recognition might have been necessary due to our limited numbers. Now, illustrious individuals, like Dr. Benbrika (may he rest in peace), who compiled the most extensive encyclopedia of Sufism, as my disciple, bore testimony numerous times in television to the impact of this path. Scholars such as Yousef Casewit, a professor of Islamic Studies at the University of Chicago, have also taken *bay`a* with me, this humble servant. Why do these accomplished individuals, with their academic prowess, choose to follow me? This question should weigh heavily on your minds, O heedless disciples.

Understand, doubtful disciple, that removing your *subḥa* and *muraqqa`a* is a challenge for a reason. I dare say that if you were to venture beyond our Tariqa, you would find yourself immersed in a sea of *waswasa*, incessant whispers that would torment you endlessly. You remind me of another disciple, a bank director in Casablanca, who, much like you, departed for the other branch but ultimately returned, burdened with remorse. He offered a significant *fidya* as an act of contrition to be readmitted to the Tariqa.

Reflect on this for a moment: I dare say I can bring individuals from China tomorrow to sit before me. I could nurture them, endow them with spiritual submission (*taslīm*), and impart knowledge unto them. However, you, heedless disciples, would remain ensnared by your *waswasa*, struggling to gain true spiritual insight, while they would progress swiftly on the path. Your cure lies in confronting these doubts in the physical realm rather than keeping them concealed within your hearts.

To free yourself from the shackles of doubt, immerse yourself in its presence in the physical realm. Recall what you've heard in Fes regarding the significance of other branches deserving your attention. Embark on this journey of self-discovery and seek Allah's ﷻ *ma`rifa*. However, bear in mind that the other branch you hold dear does not grasp the profound depths of the Divine Name or its secrets.

Their leader never truly recognized his father's worth during his lifetime. Ask the disciple ibn Sini; he will recount that when I was in *Khulwa* at Hajj Al-Hassan's house, he engaged in forbidden activities with the self-proclaimed Shaykh while ridiculing my commitment to entering *Khulwa* and seeking repentance from Allah ﷻ. Yet, that same individual now lays claim to being a Shaykh. ibn Sini attests to the misguided choices he made while simultaneously testifying about the fruitful outcomes of my *Khulwa*.

Know that our detractors remember us while we remain devoted to the remembrance of Allah ﷻ, immersed in the tranquil radiance of our spiritual journey. Comprehend that you, O heedless disciples, cannot bestow upon me anything. It is I who bestows spiritual blessings upon you, not the reverse. Now, contemplate this, seekers of the Real: the Tariqa will continue to gain prominence around the world, radiating its light ever brighter. More and more souls will benefit from its spiritual guidance, receiving divine illumination in both this world and the Hereafter. This is a decree from Allah ﷻ, an inescapable destiny.

As I conclude, I present you, the disciple who has harbored doubts about our spiritual authority, with a profound challenge. I shall embark on a journey to the United States, where I will gather erudite minds, welcoming them into our fold. I will forcefully make you land, you who is asking this question, into the realm of Islamic Studies. There, you will immerse yourself in my *madhhab*, not in the conventional Sufi sense, but within the sphere of *Usūl al-Fiqh*. This madhhab will serve as a bridge between *sharīa`a* and *ḥaqīqa*, marking the birth of the fifth madhhab. On those days, you may find yourself overwhelmed with remorse, acknowledging, "I once sat with this Shaykh without comprehending his true worth."

This, O disciples, is a challenge. If this endeavor does not come to fruition, you may assert that I am not a genuine *Walī*, that I do not rightfully inherit the legacy of the Prophet ﷺ, and even cast doubt upon the existence of his progeny.

4.
The Chosen Ones of Allah

They are the ones, those very special ones, that Allah ﷻ Himself has mentioned and spoken about, and about whom He gracefully and with divine wisdom, descended the verse: **"Patience is what you must have by being with those who call upon their Lord in the morning and the evening, desiring only His face, and don't let your eyes overlook them."**[4]

Imagine, if Allah ﷻ Himself has commanded to draw near to these people, the people of praise, the people of the *ḥamd*, what an esteemed and honored group they must be. These are the ones, the chosen ones, to whom Allah ﷻ has generously granted the inner, spiritual knowledge, *ma`rifa*.

Could you possibly think that He would grant them this profound wisdom and then hide Himself from them?

Could you conceive that the Lord, the creator of all, could bestow *ma`rifa* upon someone and then not be perpetually present with that person?

Do you perhaps think these are mere scholars who study at the well-known university of al-Azhar? That

....

4   Sūra 18. Al-Kahf, verse 28.

they just travel there, earn their degrees, and then simply return to Morocco?

No, this is not about academia. Here, we speak of the Lord. The divine presence never escapes the hearts and sights of these people, not even for a fleeting moment of a blink of an eye. If you are in the company of these people, know that you are in the presence of Allah ﷻ. Should you be fortunate enough to find such an extraordinary person, cling to them with all your might, with all your strength, and make sure not to leave their side until you have reached your spiritual goal, or until death comes to you.

You may not even be aware of the profound reality of those you are with. Reflect upon the ant that spoke to Sayyiduna Sulaymān ﷷ, causing him to pause his foot from touching the ground, to listen intently to its words, and to smile a smile imbued with the secret of *ma`rifa*. Reflect upon the teachings of the Sunna, where the Messenger of Allah ﷺ has explicitly forbidden the killing of the ant, the bee, the frog, the hoopoe, and the shrike.

Even if an ant were to bite you, you must not kill it. Rather, you should fall into prayer and prostration in grateful acknowledgment, for even in this small act of nature, modern scientists have found healing and strengthening properties for the skin and its natural defenses. Consider the bee, the shrike, the hoopoe; they have their unique attributes. Did Prophet Sulaymān ﷷ kill the hoopoe? No, he did not. To threaten the hoopoe, to intimidate it, that is different from killing it. Did he kill the ant? No, he did not. And yet, what about you?

You have killed your Shaykh. Here lies the greatest tragedy, the ultimate calamity...

Prophet Sulaymān ﷺ did not harm the hoopoe or the ant. He did not speak ill of them or slander them when they were not present. But you, you have done this very thing to your Shaykh...

5.
Wake Up: *Wilāya* Is not the Station of *Iḥsān*, and a *Walī* Does not Worship Allah "as if He Sees Him!"

In the famous hadith, after Sayyiduna Umar ﷺ questioned the Prophet ﷺ about the man who had been asking him questions and confirming the answers, he was told, "It is the angel Jibrīl ﷺ who came to teach you your religion." This statement holds a subtlety that is often overlooked.

The words that Angel Jibrīl ﷺ came to teach the religion imply that Jibrīl ﷺ himself had learned it from the Messenger of Allah ﷺ. In terms we might better understand, he is like the top student in the class, acting like a conduit sent to you specifically to teach you about the "matter" (*amr*) of your religion. The process of asking questions and receiving their answers is likened to a disciple coming with an understanding of a religious verse and seeking confirmation. If the Shaykh agrees, the disciple is reassured. If the Shaykh disagrees, the disciple must retrace his steps and correct his understanding.

This is the true reason for this interaction that occurred with Sayyiduna Jibrīl ﷺ. He was confirming what he had learned and descended from the Prophetic essence of Ahmad ﷺ by asking questions and simultaneously confirming Prophet Muhammad's ﷺ answers. That is why and how he was sent to teach the companions (not the Prophet ﷺ) their religion, but note, only to the Companions!

Consider why the Messenger of Allah ﷺ did not count himself among those learning. Why didn't he say, "It's the angel Jibrīl عليه السلام who came to teach us our religion?" This points to the fact that the teacher is the Messenger of Allah ﷺ, not Jibrīl عليه السلام. Jibrīl's عليه السلام role is to teach you about *al-Islam*, *al-Īmān*, and *al-Iḥsān*. Now, a question that might arise in the minds of many disciples is: What is *Wilāya* then?

Wilāya is more than just a part of the religion (*dīn*); it is its source and spirit. It isn't even aligned with *al-Iḥsān*. Let me clarify: *Wilāya* is not synonymous with the station of *al-Iḥsān*! *Al-Iḥsān* is a specific spiritual level within the broader context of religion (*dīn*). It's one of several stations within the spiritual journey (*sulūk*), alongside *al-Islam* and *al-Īmān*. But *wilāya* is different; it's a profound secret (*sirr*)!

In the hadith *qudsī* of the *Walī*, the Real unveils a deeper insight. It does not state, "My servant draws near to Me with extra acts of devotion until he perceives My presence everywhere." Rather, it says: "until I become his hearing, his sight, his hand, his foot." Another narration even adds: "his tongue, his eyes, his ear." So, what becomes of the person described in the hadith? He loses all sense of self, becoming a secret. He doesn't worship Allah ﷺ as if he sees Him; he transcends that level, advancing beyond the stations of the spiritual journey (*sulūk*). He loses all individual faculties, completely vanishing.

Even the statement "When he calls upon Me, I answer him" takes on new meaning. With what can he call upon Him if his tongue is no longer his? The Real, therefore, calls upon Himself by Himself. The hadith is clear about this, yet sometimes, even as we try to accept these teachings, we may find ourselves in subtle denial…

6.
Spiritual Opening (*fatḥ*) Is to See the `*Itra*

Allah ﷻ created the entirety of creation in the blink of an eye (*lamḥi baṣar*). And in reference to this, we speak of *lamḥa.* This brilliant star (*al-kawkab al-durriy*) that you witness, we refer to it as *lamḥa,* for in the realm of realities (*ḥaqīqa*), the *kawkab al-durriy* is not a mere physical planet (*kawkab*).

When we mention *lamḥa,* we are referencing the fleeting moment required for a disciple to experience the spiritual opening (*fatḥ*). Just as the awakening of this inner vision can happen in the brief duration of a blink (*lamḥi baṣar*), it can also close in the same fleeting instant. And while, from a human perspective, ten years might seem lengthy—especially if one's vision has slowly faded until total blindness—it's worth noting that in the eyes of the Divine, these ten years are as brief as a single blink.

Therefore, when we tell a disciple that we're going to grant him the *lamḥa,* we essentially convey our intent to enlighten him about the speed of the spiritual opening (*fatḥ*). Now, when we recite the verse: **"Indeed, those who pledge allegiance to you, in reality, pledge**

allegiance to Allah,"[5] we are uttering the *risāla*. But why this specific verse? It's because the one about to take this pledge (*bay`a*) is akin to a walking calamity. He lacks understanding of both intention (*niyya*) and the complete surrender to the Shaykh (*taslīm*). He is largely clueless about the essence of *bay`a*. For this reason, we impose a legal status from the *sharī`a* (*ḥukm shar`ī*) upon him, offering clear and direct evidence that he can grasp. After reciting this Quranic verse, and once we've completed the section concerning the *risāla*, we transition to discussing the *naba'*. In essence, we clarify for him that what he perceives, i.e. the star of luminous brilliance (*al-kawkab al-durriy*), is rooted in the *malakūt*.

But Honestly, we could do without all these formalities. No need to recite a single verse or even touch your hand. If the disciple is prepared, having cast away all negative thoughts, merely by approaching us, he can behold the lamp (*miṣbāh*) of the *ahl al-bayt*. This is the essence of the *fatḥ*!

What is the spiritual opening (*al-fatḥ*)?

Fatḥ is to arrive at the `itra. If someone reaches and beholds the `itra of the Prophet ﷺ, then truly, that is the *fatḥ*! This protocol that we've established exists because the one who comes here is initially lost, and when he approaches us, we need to engage with him according to his level of understanding. We need to progress with him gradually step by step.

....

5   Sūra 48. Al-Fath, verse 10.

Yet, what might such a person assume about himself? He might think that simply by following the procedure and reciting a specific verse that the spiritual mechanism was put in motion and he achieved his aim. However, this isn't true. He has recited these verses many times before without any effect. The recitation of the *bay`a's* verse is just a means (*wasīla*); it's not the end, which is to say, it isn't the *fatḥ*. The truth is, to secure the *bay`a*, you could simply come to me and tell me you pledge *bay`a*. I'd then confirm that yes, you have pledged *bay`a* to me: once you've seen me and I've recognized your *bay`a*, that's all there is. Keep up with your five daily prayers, do your *wird*[6], and that's all. Hearing this from the Shaykh is enough.

....

6   The *wird* of the Tariqa Karkariya has been added as reference at the end of the book.

7.

**Any Deed that Is not Associated
with the `*Itra* Is not Virtuous.**

If you do not possess the spiritual knowledge (*ma`rifa*) of the unique and singular *alif*, the *alif* that is not bound by any other letter, how can you understand it? The only way to know this *alif* is by binding it to the *lām*, and then it is read as "*āl*" (ال).

It is through this *āl* that the divine names became known and defined (`*urrifat*). Without the *al*, names remain undefined, hence unknown. This is what distinguishes *al-ḥakīm* from *ḥakīm*, or *al-samī`* from *samī`*, or *al-mutakallim* from *mutakallim*. Meaning, without *al*, you can attribute these names to beings, and say that so-and-so is *mutakallim* (articulate), that so-and-so is *samī`* (listener), and that so-and-so is *ḥakīm* (wise)... right? However, when you add the alif and the *lām* to these names, they no longer describe beings, but rather denote the names of the Creator Himself.

So, you—yes, you who do not recognize the *āl*, meaning you who acknowledge the Book of Allah ﷻ but not the `*itra*—know that they cannot be separated, as per the hadith. Once you separate the `*itra* from the Book,

45

you find yourself in turmoil, in a state of division (*faṣl*), descending into darknesses.

But if, conversely, you manage to connect the Book (the *alif*) to the *lām al-`ishq*, then it's as if you've unified "*āl*," and then, and only then, you can know what comes after *al*. Meaning, you might have the attribute of *ḥakīm* (wise), and through the *āl*, you attain *al-ḥakīm* (the Wise), that is, *ḥakīm* becomes *mu`arraf* (known, definite, or preceded by the determinant "the").

So, if you want to be among those possessing *ma`rifa*—oh you, the unaware… oh you, the spiritually dead, whose death has no purpose, for if only you had undergone a spiritual and initiatory death—if you want to attain true knowledge and feel intrinsically alive and existent, the only way is by binding yourself to the Book and the `*itra*. And if you fail to bind yourself to them, you will gain nothing. Absolutely nothing! You are bereft of *ta`rīf*, and all that's left is *nakira* (undefined).[7]

You, however, with all your deeds—even if you dedicate your days to what you believe are virtuous and pious actions—think of them as virtuous (*ṣālih*) deeds. But in reality, they are not.

When can a deed truly be considered virtuous?

Only when it is connected, as we have explained, to the *alif* and the *lām*.

Therefore, how can one determine if their action is *ṣālih* or not?

----

7   This implies that your name loses the determinant "*al*" that lets you shift from the attributes of the creations to those of the Creator.

It is the Lord Himself who enlightens us... not me. He declares in the hadith *qudsī*: "I fell ill and you did not visit Me. I was hungry and you did not feed Me." These are deeds. If these deeds are associated with the *lām* of "so-and-so (*fulān*)," they are virtuous deeds (*ṣālih*). If not, they are not virtuous.

Why? Because the hadith is clear: "My servant so-and-so (*fulān*) fell ill and you did not visit him. Had you visited him, you would have found Me there." The deeds mentioned here are those associated with the *lām* of "*fulān*." Your entire journey should therefore be centered on approaching the *alif* through this *lām*.

8.

The *Bay`a*: The Prophet's Example

It is crucial to comprehend one thing: it is impossible for us to objectively judge anything based solely on our rationality, as our intellect is not neutral. It is subjective and subservient to our environment, our inherited beliefs, and our perception of spiritual progression. To reject something that our intellect cannot accept is non-sensical for one who seeks the Divine. The correct disposition is to understand that our perspective—born from a darkened heart and a confined intellect—is corrupted. Therefore, it's essential to wholly relinquish it and submit fully to Allah ﷻ and His Messenger ﷺ.

This is why we emphasize the supreme importance of observing what our Beloved Prophet ﷺ has said and done; spiritual progression must always be modeled on his supreme example. The inner states, trials, and spiritual experiences he attested to must be tasted and lived by all those who tread this path. Merely following his physical Sunna is not enough. While it's mandatory, it remains insufficient. To follow the Prophet's ﷺ body without his heart suggests glaring incompleteness, if not an indicator of hypocrisy and perversion.

This sentiment is echoed by our Imam Mālik ﷺ when he states, "Whoever applies the law without Sufism is

49

a transgressor (*man tasharra`a wa lam yataḥaqqaq fa-qad tafassaq*)." Here, we must understand that anyone who physically enacts what the Messenger of Allah ﷺ prescribed—that is, the Divine Law—without realizing its profound meanings and inner reality, is corrupt. The truth isn't found solely in physically following the Prophet ﷺ. This adherence must align with the Muhammadan star shining within the heart. This embodies true sincerity and represents completeness in the religion of Allah ﷻ.

Just as with all the foundations of the Path of Allah ﷻ, the *bay`a* leads the seeker to walk in the footsteps of the Beloved Prophet ﷺ until they embody a Muhammadan example, their heart becoming a lantern illuminating their universe. That's why we say the life of the Prophet ﷺ serves as a compass for hearts, guiding the seeker on their spiritual journey by attentively aligning their inner states and spiritual experiences with those of the Beloved Prophet ﷺ.

To ascertain whether the *bay`a* undertaken is in accordance with the Prophetic Sunna, we must compare our experience with that of our Prophet ﷺ. In his life, two events remind us of the *bay`a*. The first was an extraordinary experience that occurred when he was still a child living among the tribe of Bani Sā`ida.

Sayyiduna Anas ibn Mālik ﷺ reported:

> Angel Jibrīl ﷺ came to the Messenger of Allah ﷺ while he was playing with his playmates. He took hold of him, laid him down on the ground, tore open his breast, took out the heart from it, then

extracted a blood-clot out of it and said: "That was the part of Satan in you." And then he washed it with the water of Zamzam in a golden basin and then it was joined together and restored to its place. The boys came running to his mother, i.e. his nurse, and said: "Verily Muhammad has been murdered." They all rushed toward him (and found him all right) His color was changed. Anas commented: "I myself saw the marks of needle on his breast."

The second experience transpired during his celestial ascension (*mi`rāj*). Sayyiduna Abū Dhar ﷺ reported that the Prophet ﷺ recounted, "In Makkah, my ceiling was opened, and Angel Jibrīl ﷺ descended, [...] opened my heart, washed it with *Zamzam* water, brought a golden vessel filled with wisdom and faith (Light), poured it into my chest, sealed it, took my hand, and elevated me to the lowest heaven."

As we have previously mentioned, the stages of the Prophet's ﷺ spiritual journey are not by accident, and these two accounts are no exception. If these have reached us, it is not merely for us to read with amazement and concurrent indifference. Instead, we must engage with them fully and consciously, interpreting them through spiritual experience (*ḥāl*) and divine knowledge (*ma`rifa*).

Like all Prophetic narratives, these two hadiths allude to one of the stages of the spiritual journey, specifically the pivotal stage of commitment, spiritual opening, and heart purification through the *wāsita* (intermediary). From these two hadiths, several observations can be made. Firstly, the indispensable role of the intermediary—in this case, Angel Jibril ﷺ—in the spiritual journey of the Beloved Prophet ﷺ. What is his function? It is to cleanse and purify the heart of Sayyiduna Muhammad ﷺ until he is entirely absorbed in the presence of his Lord.

In the first hadith, Sayyiduna Jibrīl ﷺ purified the heart by removing a dark "blood-clot". The children cried out, "Muhammad ﷺ is dead," signifying that at that moment, his lower self (*nafs*) was extinguished, so that nothing remained but Allah ﷻ. This act reflects one of the primary objectives of the true *bay`a*: to cleanse the seeker's heart and obliterate their lower self with divine light (*nūr Allah* ﷻ), ensuring it remains perpetually drawn to the Countenance of their Lord.

In the second hadith, Angel Jibril ﷺ repeated the purification process. He cleansed the Muhammadan heart, poured in a vessel filled with wisdom and light, and then elevated it to celestial realms. This act epitomizes one purpose of the *bay`a*: to suffuse the seeker's heart with the Light of the Real, removing all veils and revealing the divine reality. Guided by this *wāsita*, you will ascend to the first heaven, marking the entrance to the Supreme Name "Allah ﷻ," and enabling you to penetrate the sacred sanctuary of the *hā' al-hawiyya*.

9.
The Disciple and the Secret of the Shaykh

Let it be known and reflected upon, we say, that the disciple who has found his Shaykh should harbor and keep for himself the secret entrusted to him.

If the Shaykh has unveiled a secret to you, it is because he has held affection for you. He has drawn you near, distinguished you from the others, and has perceived in you all the goodness that the world can contain. As such, he has desired that you ascend to a responsibility within the station of *wilāya*.

Whether or not you prove worthy of this responsibility is not the question—it is simply because he has loved you. And in this love, he has bestowed upon you signs, given proofs, made clear the evidences, and unveiled matters to your understanding. However, should you then go and spread these matters to others, you have committed an act of apostasy.

Behold, you have transgressed!

The act of revealing the secret is one that causes its inherent benefit to evaporate. So, when does the Light become beneficial to you? When does it conquer the darkness and obliterate all obstacles? It is before this act of revelation. Shaykh al-Alawi (*Quddisa Sirruh*) has stated it in similar terms: "when an individual unveils the secret, the luminous force is withdrawn from him, and the secret is lost to him. He may even reach the point where he believes that the secret he possesses is nothing of a secret at all."

This disciple begins to doubt!

Time continues its inexorable march, and there arrives a day when the spiritual lights depart from him. He then begins to doubt even the Light itself. It is in this manner that a disciple might one day tell you that what he sees is nothing but a reflection in the retina.

But do not be deceived; it is not with your eyes that you see, but with your heart! Tear out your eyes, replace them with stones and soil, and still, you will continue to witness the Light of Allah ﷻ. When you are told, at the moment of taking the *bay`a*, to concentrate on the vision with your eyes closed, then with them open, it is because it is known in advance that you are of simple understanding, lacking in comprehension. Your inclination to trust more in physical things than in spiritual and profound meanings and manifestations is well recognized.

In response to this tendency, the Light has been shaped into a tangible form that aligns with the visual perception of the eyes. This is not a mere abstraction; the Light has been made so concrete and real that it unifies with your physical sight. This deliberate arrangement of the exemplifications of the divine Light enables you to see it even with your eyes open. By experiencing the Light in a way that appeals to your physical senses, you are able to lend credence to what you witness, bridging the gap between the tangible world and the profound spiritual truths.

10.
The Essence of Al-Ḥaqq

In the realm of realities or *ḥaqā'iq*, *Al-Ḥaqq*, the Absolute Truth, the Real, may He be exalted, holds a unique and unparalleled position. This position can be likened to the role of the number one among all numbers. Whether you are considering two, three, four, or any other number, you will find that its essence always returns to one. For instance, the number two can be understood as 1+1, three as 1+1+1, and so on.

This analogy also applies to *Al-Ḥaqq*, glorious and exalted is He, as He is the underlying reality of every level, form, and dimension in the entire universe. This is the case regardless of any apparent differences in colors, shapes, or names. Shaykh al-Alawi (*Quddisa Sirruh*) encapsulates this profound insight in one of his aphorisms: "It is not merely about recognizing Him through the multitude of His Beautiful Names. Rather, it's about knowing Him in every single sound that is uttered and every profound meaning that is conveyed. Allah said: **"And He taught Adam the names of all things"**.[8]

....

8   Sūra 2. Al-Baqara, verse 31

To recognize Him in every uttered sound implies an awareness of Him in every vibration of sound, whether it resonates from oneself or from others. It means that through the very phenomenon of sound, one can connect to an uncreated and eternal Reality. Therefore, while the forms may differ in appearance, color, and name, their essential truth is none other than *Al-Ḥaqq* Himself.

People's nature tends to limit and define the reality of things to thoughts and ideas that are created and finite. They then accept these intellectual constraints as the ultimate truth. If someone were to challenge this by saying that what has been conceptualized through the bounded intellect is not truly real but rather an illusion, feelings of denial, resentment, and even anger might arise.

The levels related to the Essence of the Divine are not fixed stages with academically defined statuses. Rather, they are expressions, like waves within the ocean. All the divine predicates (*aḥkām*) move and evolve within this Essence, akin to the waves in the ocean. By simply declaring the ocean as water, one is not contradicting reality. However, isn't there more to this water? What about its vastness, its waves, and its unique characteristics? To merely say that the ocean is water reveals a lack of deep understanding of the subject.

Ma`rifa resides in the varying degrees of the readings of the Name "Allah ﷻ" (those that come after the first Secret of *hā'*). *Ḥaqīqa* can be found in every individual. It's a universally accessible reality, accepted by all who embark on the spiritual path: everyone knows the ocean is water. This fact is known not only to humans but also to fish, animals, mountains—all creation! But what about the sciences of the ocean itself? The understanding related to its tides, its vastness, the specific characteristics of its depths and surfaces, the variations in temperature, its level of salinity—all of this speaks to the multifaceted sciences of its different degrees emerging after acknowledging the fundamental truth that the ocean is indeed water.

11.
Blossoming in Solitude:
The Importance of Spiritual Detachment

Seekers of divine light, a friend from America approached me, wanting to know how to avoid distractions on his journey to connect with Allah ﷻ. I explained to him that true detachment is not merely physical—it begins deep within our souls. For those new to this journey, it's essential to tread cautiously at the outset. Steer clear of individuals and certain Sufi books that might act as veils, obscuring the truth and leading you astray. Additionally, be mindful of devices like phones and tablets; they can easily distract you in this journey.

O new disciples, understand that at the outset of this sacred expedition, you are akin to green fruits, yet to ripen in your knowledge of Allah ﷻ, unable to fully discern between the virtuous and the malevolent, or ascertain who is close to or distant from Allah's ﷻ grace. To foster both personal growth and spiritual fortification, I advise you, O novices, to find sanctuary primarily within your homes during the initial phases of your spiritual exploration. This sanctuary is not merely a physical structure but should be a haven where you can immerse yourselves in deep contemplation and remembrance of Allah ﷻ, shielded from misleading external influences. During this time, let your hearts seek guidance exclusively from your Shaykh, your spiritual mentor who graced you with his knowledge and nurtured your spirits. Immerse yourself in the divine remembrance until Allah ﷻ unveils a fresh horizon for you.

I urge you, O heedless disciples, to walk in the footsteps of the revered Mother Maryam عليها السلام, whose devotion and seclusion are reported in the Quran. This path of solitude should not be misconstrued as a neglect of one's familial responsibilities. Nay, interactions must adhere to the boundaries delineated by the *sharīa`a* to prevent you, O novice, from entangling yourself in complex and unbearable circumstances. Know that this initial passage should be characterized by solitude and seclusion. It should be a phase of deep engagement with *dhikr* and remembrance of Allah ﷻ.

In this phase, I encourage you to cultivate a conscious detachment from worldly affairs and the concerns of others. Recognize the years mired in negligence and sin. This should foster in you an authentic desire to reshape your lives to align more closely with Allah's ﷻ revered teachings, guided by the wisdom of your Shaykh and the principles of his Tariqa. Reflect on the monumental Day of Judgment, a moment where each soul will stand solitary, accountable for her deeds. This should ignite in you a fervent motivation to traverse this path in solitude, shunning those who do not merit your attention.

O seekers of the Real, traversing the path of spiritual illumination, understand that this journey is oftentimes misinterpreted, with critics hastily branding the disciples as being shrouded in depression or marred by mental unrest. Yet, in essence, this is but a spiritual longing, a fervent desire to foster closeness with Allah ﷻ, with the sole respite found in the ceaseless remembrance of the Almighty. In this sacred undertaking, I serve as a spiritual healer, dispensing the necessary cures to guide you, be it through solitude or integration within the community, all in accordance to your stage of spiritual realization. My guidance is a luminescent beacon, aiding disciples in steering through the intricacies of their spiritual voyage, warding off potential hostilities and hardships as elucidated in the Quranic verses concerning friendship and belief.

O, wayfarers, it is vital to cultivate a demeanor of humility, recognizing your finite comprehension and embracing the sanctity of solitude. Regrettably, many embark on this journey burdened with prior connections and affiliations that, alas, hinder the process of spiritual liberation and realization. It becomes an urgent necessity for those individuals to engage more actively in the process of detachment, relying upon divine grace to shepherd it to fruition.

At the heart of this metamorphosis lies the mastery over one's tongue, a potential source of spiritual decline, but also a potent instrument for spiritual ascent through *dhikr*. In this age, many souls are drawn to rampant verbosity, a tendency that must be curbed to foster genuine spiritual growth. I recall tales from my initial journey to my Shaykh, Hajj Al-Hassan, where I relinquished all my worldly possessions that might have been acquired through unsanctioned means, all in pursuit of profound repentance to Allah ﷻ.

As you immerse yourselves in this transformative expedition, it is necessary to break bonds with acquaintances that epitomize modern friendships, forging a fertile ground for earnest engagement in *dhikr*. It perplexes me, how individuals in this era sustain thousands of friendships in social media when, in bygone times, we found fulfillment with a mere ten or twenty intimate companions. I ponder, how do you navigate existence amidst this relentless tide of interactions, emerging gadgets, and an infinite cascade of books awaiting perusal? I reflect that in my time, attention was devoted to a select few, profound manuscripts. I question you, disciples, where do you unearth the time for these diversions? When do you submerge yourselves in the profound remembrance of Allah ﷻ? Genuine immersion in *dhikr* seems elusive amidst this prevailing tumult that you self-imposed on yourself.

O, disciples, reflect upon my personal journey, you will discover in it a wellspring of inspiration in my unwavering dedication to *dhikr* and my firm resolve to establish a more intimate connection with the Divine Presence. It is pertinent for me to emphasize that my intention in sharing these personal narratives is not to vent, but to humbly convey the teachings granted to me in my role as a *Walī*, entrusted by Allah ﷻ to shepherd you on this spiritual voyage. I am, whether you accept or not, a beacon of luminous guidance, whose radiant light, manifested profoundly within your hearts, is experienced in the palpable reality, not confined to mere metaphors. I recount episodes of deep remembrance, moments where I dedicated countless hours, my forehead embracing the walls, enveloped in the profound silence surrounding my *dhikr*, shielding myself from the tempting distractions of the outside world. Driven by an unquenchable desire for closeness to Allah ﷻ and the unveiling of secrets hidden beyond the luminous manifestations, I offered myself with undivided passion to this divine journey. While the world swayed in its perpetual dance around me, my father partaking in his day-to-day activities, I stood resolute engrossed in the harmonious resonance of my *dhikr*.

Seeking the quietude of secluded corners within the big mosque of Al-Aroui to elude distractions, I nurtured a deep and personal communion with the Divine Luminescence, a light that, as if by divine orchestration, magnetically drew souls towards me. Observe this paradox, heedless disciples, that as you get closer to the divine light and carve distance from others, they find themselves captivated, drawn towards your aura, yearning for your attention, your benevolent affection. Allah ﷻ, in His infinite wisdom and grace, attends to your every need, often before they crystallize in your conscious awareness, masterfully arranging encounters with beings endowed with answers to your unvoiced inquiries, guiding your footsteps with subtlety yet unequivocal certainty.

To conclude, Seekers of the Real, I impart unto you that the initial phases of this spiritual expedition are comparable to the tender nurturing of a fledgling plant, shielded diligently from potential harm until it blossoms into a mighty tree, fortified enough to withstand the corrosive influences of society, including individuals perceived to be of diminished moral stature. The emphasis during this nascent stage is to foster growth, to cultivate the light of the Real until it unfolds magnificently, commanding reverence and attracting others towards the luminous embrace of God that dwells within. Embark upon this journey with a dedicated heart, and witness the divine accompaniment guiding you towards the wisdom you ardently seek, establishing connections that spur spiritual elevation, ushering you ultimately to a sanctuary of certainty and resilience in your faith. And then, poised to reintegrate with the world, laden with the bountiful fruits of your spiritual labor and cultivation, a reborn luminous soul emerges, prepared to guide others towards the luminous path of divine light and *ma`rifa.*

12.
Navigating Spiritual Obedience

When you visit the Shaykh, you must ensure to fulfil his directives precisely. If he advises you to wear the *muraqqa`a*, obey him!

Consider the story of a tanner Shaykh. One day, he was washing skins when a disciple passed by. The Shaykh asked him to remove his shoes and help him. They toiled together, and after the Shaykh's death, the disciple himself became a Shaykh. Once, his disciples asked why he never wore shoes. He replied that he was simply obeying his Shaykh's final instruction to remove his shoes while washing the skins and since he was never told to put them back on, he continued to stay barefoot. Even as people pointed out that his Shaykh's instruction was contextual, he remained steadfast. He claimed that since his Shaykh had told him to remove his shoes, he would remain shoeless.

Yet, disciples, a certain disciple was asked to wear the *muraqqa`a*, but he repeatedly takes it off. This is despite him having brought a *muraqqa`a* and had me pray on it, signifying his commitment to wear it.

[A disciple then questioned if there were any exceptions. Sidi Shaykh (*Quddisa Sirruh*) replied:]

How do your reasons for not wearing it pertain to me?

Until now, we've discussed the foundations of the spiritual journey. However, if you wish to discuss reasons not to do certain things, understand that I have never explicitly instructed anyone to wear the *muraqqa`a*. The day I donned it, I did so for myself. And when I removed it, it was also for my own reasons. My actions and my prayers serve my personal relationship with my Lord. It's up to the disciples behind me to choose their own paths. They should follow the Imam, not expect the Imam to follow them.

Some disciples may not perform the prayer correctly or follow my method of praying, but I never point this out. It's on them to demonstrate wisdom and understanding. If they argue, "But the Shaykh didn't tell me to do this or that…" these individuals are, according to the masters of this art, disrespecting the sanctity of the mosque. This is why Sufi poetry urges disciples to observe their Shaykh, because it's their role to observe, not the Shaykh's to instruct every detail. The Shaykh is there for disciples to follow. So, emulate his actions, whether you comprehend the reasoning or not. During open discussions, feel free to ask: "Sidi Shaykh (*Quddisa Sirruh*), we saw you do this and that, what does that mean?" That's the appropriate time for inquiries. If he doesn't invite questions, retain his actions in your heart. Simply practice what you saw and if asked why, reply that you are emulating the Prophet's ﷺ descendant, and that suffices.

This is the essence of *bay`a*. The *bay`a* is not a casual commitment. It means, "**May I follow you,**"[9] as Sayy-

....

9   Sūra 18. Al-Kahf, verse 66.

iduna Mūsa ﷵ asked of Sayyiduna al-Khidr ﷵ in *Sūrat al-Kahf.* However, be wary; the Prophet ﷺ cautioned against taking one's *bayʿa* lightly: "Whoever retracts from obedience will meet Allah ﷻ on the Last Day with no justification. And whoever dies without a *bayʿa* around his neck, dies a death of ignorance (*mawtata al-jāhiliyya*)."

13.
Such Is the Wise (*Al-Ḥakīm*)!

When Sayyiduna al-Khidr ﷺ and Sayyiduna Mūsa ﷺ met, al-Khidr ﷺ did not just casually kill children in front of people. He did not wander the desert killing innocent people he encountered, nor did he sail the seas to sabotage ships, or built walls in towns without asking for payment. All this was done in the presence of Sayyiduna Mūsa ﷺ, for with others, he ﷺ is but an ordinary man.

Don't imagine that those versed in the Science of *ḥaqīqa* are so advanced that they are above Divine Law, and can thus contradict it at will, hiding behind the example of Sayyiduna al-Khidr ﷺ. You might object though by saying, "but al-Khidr ﷺ killed a child..." My child, when you reach the level of realization of Sayyiduna al-Khidr ﷺ, and someone like Prophet Mūsa ﷺ comes to you, then yes, manifest an esoteric sign that corresponds to his level of understanding.

Al-Khidr ﷺ performed these acts solely because Sayyiduna Mūsa ﷺ was Mashā'Allah: a Prophet, messenger, and one of the *ūlū al-`azm*. That's why when he saw al-Khidr ﷺ sabotage the ship, he objected but did not flee. When he saw him kill the child, he objected but remained with him. You, however, would flee at the start, for you are not convinced that these are signs sent directly from the Lord. You might think they are perhaps whispers of *Shaytān*, or of the self. So be cautious and remain vigilant!

The Wise (*Al-Ḥakīm*) maintains unwavering integrity in every action and word, demonstrating consistency and alignment with Divine Law. This is not a display of hypocrisy but rather a commitment to uphold righteousness, ensuring that those who follow are not led astray or disturbed by contradictions.

The Wise (*Al-Ḥakīm*) possesses a profound understanding that enables them to discern between the Light and the forces of darkness. This discernment is not obtained through superficial practices performed merely for outward appearance, devoid of inner truth. Instead, it is acquired by the seeker through a deep comprehension of the sciences of *ḥaqīqa*, an understanding rooted in the spiritual reality conveyed by celestial messages and clear revelations. This wisdom goes beyond mere surface-level intellectual knowledge, reflecting a true engagement with the spiritual principles and truths that these messages emanating from the world of the unseen contain.

14.
Your Heart Is Rusted
by Your Heedlessness (*ghafla*)!

On that Day, it will be of absolutely no use to know what someone else has done or to be able to read others' thoughts—you won't be questioned about that! Rather, you will be questioned about your compliance with the Law: Have you acted with fairness in your journey, have you faithfully adhered to the path of the Prophet ﷺ? The Messenger of Allah tells us in a hadith, "This is the Way of Allah ﷻ; follow it, and do not follow the paths that deviate from it." This is what you will be questioned about on the Day of Judgment.

Here is where the true essence of religion must guide you in your earthly life, enabling you to lift the veil that obscures the Creator's presence. By recognizing the mark of the Creator flowing through all things, you become an eyewitness to this profound truth. This is not merely an intellectual understanding but a concrete spiritual experience that reveals the essence (*jawhar*), spirit (*rūḥ*), and taste (*dhawq*) of religion.

This will strengthen your faith, your certainty, and your attachment to religion—or rather, to the essence of religion, to the spirit of religion, to the taste of religion. You will then perform prayers, fasting, and all your worship, savoring each one. Outwardly, you will do neither more nor less than an ordinary Muslim, but you will surpass this ordinary person through Knowledge, when the true flavor of worship is unveiled to you.

Therefore, when the time for prayer comes, you will not rise lazily or indifferently. It won't be a burden on your heart; instead, it will be a source of nearness (*qurb*) and revival. Hence, if you notice a heaviness in your heart when performing worship, your *wird*, prayer, or fasting, know that you must return to examining the reality of your heart and to imploring Divine Forgiveness (*istighfār*) so that your disturbances fade and the rust that has affected your heart disappears.

If you had truly tasted the flavor of worship, the veil would have been lifted. Don't claim to be among those whose veil has been lifted if you are lazy in your worship! Those whose veil has been lifted are always foremost in the worship of the Lord. This mystical experience of unveiling is accessible through certainty (*yaqīn*), Love, and the firm and final establishment of the mirror of the heart after it has been duly polished and stripped of its inclinations towards this world's trivialities. For as Sayyiduna al-Mustafa ﷺ teaches us, "hearts rust like iron, and they are polished by the remembrance (*dhikr*) of Allah ﷻ."

Why by the remembrance of Allah ﷻ?

Simply because the cause of the hearts' rusting is heedlessness (*ghafla*). The absence of *dhikr* leads to heedlessness and inclination towards the passions of the self, hence a state of distance. Most of you, disciples, find the gatherings of *dhikr* heavy and burdensome.

What does that mean? That means that your heart is rusted! Even if you come to us claiming to see wonders and extraordinary visions, we cannot believe you; you are not reliable, for when you sit with us, you are not present...

15.
Mark these Words: Divine Light Shines Beyond the Illusions of the Mind!

The Highest Level of Vision: The visualization of the fourfold Exemplifications of Allah's Light:

O heedless disciples, reflect upon the profound words: **"Allah is the Light of the heavens and the earth."**[10] Understand that during your *dhikr*, you may perceive what exists within the heavens and the earth. But those among you who witness the Divine Light are at a more advanced level. In fact, this Light represents the reality of all creatures confined within the heavens and the earth. Know, disciple, that the vision of the Light is a crucial and profound aspect of our journey. Allah ﷻ has exemplified this Light through four examples. He described it as a niche, wherein is a lamp; the lamp is in a glass, and the glass is as if it were a shining star.

In wayfaring, your main objective must be to attain the knowledge of Allah ﷻ through the steps prescribed by Him. Beware of following paths that might lead you astray. When you see the niche, and then move to the vision of the lamp and the glass, arriving at the shining star, know that this is a higher level than merely observ-

....

10   Sūra 24. An-Nur, verse 35.

ing the creatures of the heavens and the earth. The heavens are vast and limitless; two consecutive heavens are separated by a distance that takes 500 years to traverse, as the Prophet ﷺ teaches us. If you focus solely on the images of what is contained within the heavens and the earth, you may perish before even comprehending what lies within the first heaven, let alone the second, third, and beyond. Thus, you must concentrate on what leads you to know the Creator of all creatures, not the creatures themselves. This is the path we walk, and this is the knowledge we seek. Let your focus be on the Divine Light, the shining star, and the Creator, and let your vision be clear and pure.

How to Differentiate Between Illusions and the Vision of the Divine Light:

O heedless disciples, I must draw your attention to a matter of importance. In our Tariqa, we find an increasing involvement of scientific minds, while at the same time, others from outside the Tariqa engage in research and investigations concerning the vision of the Divine Light. You may hear some researchers suggesting that the visions of the Divine Light experienced by you, the seekers, are merely optical reflections—images perceived when you sit down, close your eyes in a tranquil place, reflecting upon your sight.

Allow me to clarify this misconception. If these visions were merely optical reflections, they would remain constant; they would not change in size, getting neither bigger nor smaller. Simple optical reflections would not offer a comprehensive understanding and display of the various stages of creation, from its beginning to its ulti-mate completion. If this were the case, all of humanity would rely on mere optical reflections to understand how Allah ﷻ brought everything into existence, aban-doning the opening of the eye of the spirit (*baṣīra*) that leads us to the concrete spiritual visualization of Allah's ﷻ vast creation.

So, how do you differentiate reality from illusions of the *nafs*? It is simple: if what you see aligns with the Sunna, it cannot be associated with mere imagination or optical reflections. But if it does not correspond to what Allah ﷻ the Almighty has transmitted through the words of the Prophet ﷺ, then you have the right to ques-tion and criticize what you perceive. Always remember, the benchmark is the *sharī`a*. This is our path to dis-tinguish reality from illusion and imagination.

Lastly, be aware that illusions and imaginations do exist, and they are considered an illness within the mind. It is our duty to cure and purify these afflictions, align-ing ourselves with what is found in the Quran and Sunna. Let your vision be clear, your mind pure, and your heart aligned with the Truth.

Tariqa Karkariya: A Scientific Approach Based on the Sciences of the Prophet ﷺ:

O heedless disciples, today I will speak to you about different types of visions within our Tariqa. It's not simply about seeing what is hidden in the universe. What we follow is a scientific approach. But by "scien-tific," I don't mean the sciences of physics or biology; I mean the Prophetic Ahmadian Divine ones.

Our path is centered around the fourfold exemplifications of The Divine Light. Know, O disciple, that if you ground these exemplifications in your heart, then you will possess a key to enter the Blessed Tree (*ash-shajara al-mubāraka*). Knowing and appreciating this fact leads us to magnify the examples of the Divine Light. Reflect upon the vastness of the heavens and the earth. Both are physical manifestations, made up of elemental components: soil, air, fire, and water. Yet, beyond their tangible form, there's a divine essence that binds and enlightens them. When Allah ﷻ sought to explain the nature of His Light, He revealed to us that this very Light is the source from which all matter and existence spring forth. Even us humans, we exist because of Allah's ﷻ Light.

Reflect upon the human body. You may perceive it as merely flesh, fat, and blood, but this view does not encompass the true essence of *al-Insān*. What you observe physically is but the lowest manifestation of humanity, a trace produced by the Divine Light. Conventional science, with its focus on the tangible, is limited to capturing only this superficial aspect, unable to penetrate the profound spiritual reality that underlies our existence.

Try to perceive, O ignorant one, humans not merely as flesh, bones, and fat, but instead as spiritual creations. Consider what Allah ﷻ has instilled within each person: how we come into existence, live for a period on earth, transition to the grave, then to the isthmus (*barzakh*), the Day of Resurrection, and ultimately to eternal life in paradise or hell. Reach and realize yourself in this understanding, and you have attained a level of knowledge. Otherwise, remain veiled from Allah's ﷻ bestowed wisdom.

Understanding the human body as a mere machine, as robots, overlooks the most significant part of a human: the Divine breath (*nafkha rūḥia*), which leads to the knowledge of Allah ﷻ and His contemplation and direct witnessing. And know that if you see humans as only physical beings without recognizing their spiritual dimension, you will never attain knowledge of Allah ﷻ. Remember, there are people with high academic degrees who still prostrate before rocks and cows. What benefit is there in their worldly sciences and knowledge if it doesn't help them realize that we are creatures created by Allah ﷻ? If your knowledge doesn't lead you to worship Allah ﷻ in the way He desires, what purpose does it serve?

So, if your academic knowledge leads you to know the Creator, then your knowledge becomes a steed for you to the Divine Presence and is considered useful and genuine knowledge. Otherwise, it cannot be considered knowledge at all.

Conclusion:

Consider again, o disciple, the verse: **"Allah is the Light of the heavens and the earth."**

Let us reflect on its profound meanings. When Allah ﷻ declared these words, He meant with them all of His creations found in the heavens and the earth. He wanted us to ponder and meditate on the very fabric of our existence and realize that our essential origin is Light.

If, in our reflections and meditations, we fail to reach this conclusion and Allah's ﷻ Light, then our reflections are in vain and are rejected.

Understand, my brethren, that this is the essence of our Tariqa. Our main objective is to know Allah ﷻ the Almighty. It's not merely about acquiring worldly titles such as engineer, doctor, or physician. Those achievements are meaningless if we do not come to know our Lord. Our path is a journey towards the Light, and it is that sacred illumination that we must strive to reach. May Allah ﷻ guide us all along this blessed path. *Amīn.*

16.
The Lord Wills that Only His Light Persists!

You, who recite **"Allah is the light of the heavens and the earth,"** present yourself at the very core of His light. But meanwhile, you wish to manifest a shape, a form, an image within it? Feel shame before Allah ﷻ, heedless disciple! Here, you observe that even on this level, you are far, very far from the *ma`rifa* of Allah ﷻ. In truth, you have not even yet set foot in the spiritual retreat (*khulwa*) while you claim you have been through it years ago.

Be cautious, as I'm speaking to you through the *lām al-qabḍ*, but I'm showing you through these teachings that you haven't even understood the *hā' al-hawiyya*. Despite your level of studies, despite your daily recitation of the Quran, despite your claims of having memorized, studied, meditated upon it—just on this subject that we have just discussed, you are far, you are very, very far.

Now, teach us about the Oneness (*tawḥīd*) of Allah ﷻ. See?! You are incapable of such a thing! Instead, He has Unified Himself, by Himself, without your creation, and without your existence. Therefore, praise your Lord, and bow to Him in a prostration of gratitude (*shukr*), for the fact that He created you. Instead of getting angry and spitting on this mundane world, thank the Lord for having brought you into existence in this world. Here, you were able to know and distinguish the Lord's immanence (*tashbīh*) from His transcendence (*tanzīh*). You were able to recognize the false misleading claims of self-proclaimed mystics and detractors alike regarding indwelling (*al-ḥulūl*) and unification (*al-ittiḥād*). You were also able to distinguish the Creator from His creation.

You, you stand as mere non-existence before the Divine Essence; you are mere nothingness, within nothingness. As for the Divine Essence itself, no words or descriptions can truly encompass it. Whatever you may attempt to say or express falls infinitely short of capturing its true nature. You have, in reality, no right to articulate or approach it except through the guidance and path shown by the Prophet ﷺ. And the Prophet ﷺ left you a mystery to unravel at *sidrat al-muntahā*, and in the seven heavens. He left you a mystery to decipher in moving from the perimeter (*iḥāta*) to the center (*markaz*), and from the center to the perimeter, completing thus the rays of a full disc rising in the Divine presence, to finally say: "You are as You have praised Yourself."[11]

After that, he returned and brought us the most flavorful of worships, the most noble bond (*ṣila*) that we call *aṣ-ṣalāt*. In our approach to this prayer (*ṣalāt*), we

....

11 This quotation is from the hadith of the *isrā'* and *mi'rāj* (Night Journey and Ascension), describing the words the Prophet ﷺ uttered at the moment he met Allah ﷻ at *Sidrat al-Muntahā*.

are often merely fulfilling an obligation (*qaḍā'*) rather than truly embodying its spiritual dimensions (*qiyām*). Consider the one who has fully established (*aqāma*) his bond with the Lord: his feet may be grounded on the earthly plane, but his forehead, in prostration, reaches *sidrat al-muntahā*, the farthest boundary. For such a person, the additional prayers (*nāfila*) take precedence over the obligatory prayers (*farḍ*). To him, the obligatory prayers are a fulfillment (*qaḍā'*), a duty met, while the additional prayers serve as a means of drawing nearer to the Most Merciful. This perspective contrasts sharply with the conventional understanding, where priorities may be considered in a reversed manner.

17.
Reflections on the Role of a Shaykh and the Company We Keep

The Shaykh, as has been stated, is the one who never ceases to polish the mirror of your heart. He polishes it until the lights of your Lord come to reflect in it, so that you may ascend to Him. When you reach that point, the Shaykh will tell you, "Here you are, you and your Lord."

Such is the Shaykh. He polishes your heart, motivating you, making you move, granting you light, and taking away your darkness, until he can say to you, "Here you are, you and your Lord." He is the one who takes you out of the realm of worldly desires and pushes you into the presence of the Lord.

Ibn `Abbās ﷺ asked in a hadith, "O Messenger of Allah ﷺ, who are the people of the best companionship?" You, who like to spend your time at the café, enjoying sweets and tea, this is our master ibn `Abbās ﷺ teaching you that you need to change and understand the spiritual condition and state (*ḥāl*) of the true seekers. Understand how to sit, with whom, and how to choose your traveling companions. The Prophet ﷺ answered, "The one whose sight reminds you of Allah ﷺ." This means that the person should be such that, just by seeing him, you remember Allah ﷻ. That is the one whose company you should seek. But if the one you associate with does not remind you of Allah ﷻ—if when you see him, you think of business, buying and selling, heedlessness (*ghafla*), or generally anything other than Allah ﷻ—abandon him.

Then, he ﷺ added, "The one whose sight reminds you of Allah ﷻ, whose speech increases you in knowledge." Meaning the one who, when he speaks, articulates in such a way that he provides you with proofs and a profound understanding, expanding your realm of knowledge. Someone who adds to the wisdom that Allah ﷻ has already placed in you.

What is this wisdom that he has added to you? It is his insight (*mantiq*). That is, he will bring you a Quranic verse, and elucidate it for you with spiritual clarity and divine comprehension, connecting it to the greater truths of existence.

Finally, the Messenger of Allah ﷺ added, "The one whose sight reminds you of Allah ﷻ, whose speech increases you in knowledge, and whose actions remind you of the Hereafter." Meaning that as soon as you learn of his deeds, it reminds you of the Hereafter.

The one you should follow must be such that his sight reminds you of Allah ﷻ, his insight enhances your knowledge, and his deeds remind you of the Hereafter. If you find such a companion, join his gathering. If not, stay by yourself, alone. Do not waver in your pursuit of spiritual companionship; seek only those who truly embody these virtues. Do not return tomorrow or the day after with indecision, questioning whether you can follow this person or that, or expressing mere worldly attachments. Focus on the divine guidance and look for those who lead you closer to Allah ﷻ and remind you of the Hereafter, not those tied to earthly concerns.

In the continuation of the hadith, it is said, "Such are the banners of praise (*al-ḥamd*)." In simple terms, these people, whose company is good to share, are the embodiment of the phrase "*al-ḥamdulillah*." When you perform your obligatory prayers, and you recite "*al-ḥamdulillah rabbi l`ālamīn*," know that it is them that you are referring to in the *ḥamdala*. They are the truth of praise. They are the people of the Lord's presence. They are those who have realized the complete abstraction from anything other than Allah ﷻ, starting with themselves, their own ego (*nafs*), before everything that surrounds them.

18.
"By the Witness
and the One who Is Witnessed"

Good news and blessings to those who have seen the light of al-Mustafa ﷺ, for this vision is nothing other than the vision of the spiritual reality of the Prophet ﷺ. The illumination of all the *Awliyā*, the Truthful ones (*ṣiddiqīn*), the Prophets, and all pure-hearted beings emanates from His lamp. He thus contemplates Himself through every witnessing person.

You say: "I see the Messenger of Allah ﷺ." But have you considered whether He sees you in return? In the physical world, sight is often reciprocal; when you see someone, they typically see you as well. However, there can be exceptions, such as when a person is blind, allowing you to see them without being seen in return. Yet, in the spiritual realm, this reciprocity is absolute. If you see the Prophet ﷺ, rest assured, He sees you too.

Know, then, and be certain, that when you see this light, when you gaze upon this supreme spirit, know that one of two things is true: either this is proof in your favor, or it's evidence against you. Because He sees you. Just as you saw Him, He saw you. Imagine then, even as you behold Allah's ﷻ light, you still commit sins, you lie, you steal, or worse. Be well aware that you committed these acts while the Messenger of Allah ﷺ was watching you! You sinned while He observed you!

Stay mindful of your actions! You might think, "I've received the Shaykh's light through the *bay`a*, then left, and now I'm free to act as I please." This is not the case! From the moment you accept the light, He is with you. He is the supreme spirit and is present with you in every moment. When you do good, He is there, witnessing in your favor. And when you err, He is there, bearing witness against you.

Thus, He observes Himself through each individual who sees Him. In other words, you perceive Him with a vision of unity (*jam`*), as if all parts are joined into a whole. Meanwhile, He sees you with a vision of dispersion (*farq*), recognizing all those who have been touched by a fragment of His original and radiant spirit.

Since we are now in the realm of *lām al-qabḍ*, if your spirit is seized (*qubiḍat*), as well as your intellect and your understanding, then He becomes the witness and the one who is witnessed. And your character (*khuluq*) becomes the character of the Prophet ﷺ.

The Messenger of Allah ﷺ commanded: "Pray as you have seen me pray." Even if you are devoted to constant prayer, seeing the Prophet ﷺ just once in your life equips you to pray in the way you witnessed Him pray. And If you find yourself in a state where your vision of the Prophet ﷺ is continuous and unbroken, understand that you are essentially in a state of perpetual prayer. This experience establishes a connection (*ṣila*) with Him. In other words, during your prayer, He becomes your imam, guiding you, and you become His follower (*ma'mūm*). You are hence in union with the Prophet ﷺ.

Known to see both behind and before Him, the Messenger of Allah ﷺ becomes both the witness and the one who is witnessed. Ultimately, it is He ﷺ who prays, and any prayer you perform holds value and is accepted only as part of His prayer. For the true prayer is none but the Prophet's ﷺ prayer. This, then, is what is referred to by the witness (*shāhid*) and the one who is witnessed (*mashhūd*) in the divine words: **"By the sky with its constellations! And by the promised day! And by the witness and the one who is witnessed!"**[12]

....

12 Sūra 85. Al-Burooj, verses 1-3.

19.

The False Modesty of the Disciple
Towards the Shaykh

The Messenger of Allah ﷺ said: "Two types of people do not learn: the shy and the arrogant."

Remember this well and firmly engrave it into your mind. The shy and the arrogant.

The arrogant will never learn. One who perceives himself to be "something" remains and always stays behind. He is fundamentally the last because arrogance (*al-kibr*) is a trait of the ultimate enemy of Allah ﷻ: *Iblīs*.

Consider now the one who is timid, the one who hesitates to step forward. It is vital to remember that Allah ﷻ and His Messenger ﷺ favor the believer who demonstrates strength. But this strength isn't defined by the ability to hoist a heavy load. Rather, it lies within the believer. It is an internal force, characterized by self-confidence and assurance. It is the wisdom to discern the appropriate times for humility and silence, and the courage to voice one's needs when necessary.

Let me tell what goes into the minds of many of you, heedless disciples, "No… I have a question… well, indeed, the Shaykh opened the door for me to ask, but I don't want to talk, I'm embarrassed… I'm practicing *adab* (good manners)." Well then, stay seated in your place. To you, *adab* has only come in the form of asking a question. However, as soon as the Shaykh leaves, you find yourself blaring like a popstar. In that moment, you no longer think of practicing *adab*!

This question you have, ask it, but with *adab*! Through this question, the one who listens to you will love you. If they understand you, they will respond. And if they don't understand you, they will love you for the *adab* you demonstrated while asking this question. Indeed, there exist individuals for whom we eagerly anticipate their words, our curiosity piqued about when they will finally break their silence. In contrast, there are those whose ceaseless chatter leaves us longing for a moment of quietness, wondering when they will finally choose silence.

There are some the Lord gives them what they ask for simply to no longer have to listen to them speak. They persistently ask, and the Lord says, "Give him what he demands, so he finally falls silent!" Because He doesn't like them. Here, you understand that granting of wishes or answered supplication are not the goal at all. The only and unique goal is the knowledge (*ma`rifa*) of the Lord. Because if your Lord fulfills your wish but He doesn't love you, what have you truly gained!?

On the other hand, there are certain individuals whose prayers are so beloved to the Lord, that He may delay answering their pleas. This is not out of neglect, but because He cherishes hearing their supplications. These servants, their words, are truly loved by Him.

As for you… you don't even speak!

We have heard nothing from you, and you have remained silent. But as soon as we leave, your dynamo springs into action, and you start speaking. So here is someone who has misunderstood the essence of *adab*. When Sayyiduna Al-Khidr عليه السلام says to Mūsa عليه السلام, "If you follow me, do not question me about anything until I myself inform you of it," it means "do not question me about anything that you perceive as being beyond your intellectual comprehension."

Naturally, when we undertake a journey together, there are bound to be queries and clarifications about our day-to-day activities. Questions like, "Will we sleep here?" or "When will we eat?" will inevitably arise. Such discussions are to be expected. However, when I perform or exhibit something that surpasses your understanding, refrain from questioning me about it. Do not demand an explanation, do not persist. Wait patiently, for when the time is right, I will provide the necessary insights.

What does this signify in practical terms for the disciple?

It denotes: never approach saying, "Sidi Shaykh, grant me permission to practice *dhikr* with the name 'Allah ﷻ'." The moment I hear such a request, your spiritual influx will be immediately severed. "Sidi Shaykh, allow me to enter into *khulwa*." With this attitude, you will never set foot in the spiritual seclusion, and never will you be privy to a secret. That's why al-Khidr عليه السلام says: "If you follow me, don't ask me anything."

This has nothing to do with questions like: "I read such verse and I believe I understood this and that… is it correct?" What you must refrain from asking is anything suggesting a hastiness to leap through the stages of your journey on this path. For instance, "Sidi Shaykh,

I've been here in the *zāwiya* for quite some time, isn't it about time you permit me to enter *khulwa*?!" or "Grant me the second secret" or "This is my interpretation of the third secret."

No! Even if you were to decipher the secret verbatim and present it on my desk, you will never succeed. Because each secret has its own rules, its own station, its own timeframe for it to be spiritually transmitted and verbalized. The Lord indeed says: **"In chambers (hearts) that Allah has permitted (*idhn*) to be raised and in which His name is mentioned."**[13] Until you receive this permission (*idhn*), and then only you can devote yourself to *dhikr*. Here, you learn to evoke (*dhikr*) the name of Allah ﷻ, accompanied by the vision of Allah's ﷻ attribute, in order to reach Allah's ﷻ essence.

In summary, this is what you are not allowed to talk about, until the *idhn* of Allah ﷻ comes. If you talk about it, you would certainly have shown a lack of *adab*. On the other hand, for things that you go through in your daily life, no, it is absolutely your right to express yourself. Ask your question, always within the limits of *adab*. But if you refuse to ask, you won't learn anything, it's as simple as that. Should you refrain from asking, your learning will be reliant on the questions posed by others. Here, you'll need to exercise sharpness and perceptiveness. The sharp and perceptive individual learns from the signs directed towards them, but also those directed towards others. However, the fool, who fails to compre-

....

13   Sūra 24. An-Nur, verse 36.

hend the signs meant for them, is unlikely to grasp those concerning others!

Yet, you often confuse perceptiveness with cunning. You perceive the one we call "sharp and perceptive" as a master of deceit. No! On one hand, there's perceptiveness, and on the other, cunning. These two shouldn't be conflated.

20.
Beware, O Murid! Do not Let the Company of Other Disciples Harm You!

We continuously urge you not to worry about others in your spiritual journey. Focus on yourself. Why? Because what matters is your own path. All your papers need to be in order. It doesn't concern you whether someone else's papers are in order or not. Everyone has their own business. What counts is that I am in order. I need to have my own visa, my own identity card. Everyone needs to look after themselves.

If you were truly concerned about your own condition, you would forget about those around you.

And why is the Shaykh indispensable here?

Simply because he is the one who helps you to get all these papers in order. He tells you which documents you are missing. That's why you show respect (*adab*) towards him and follow his requests, because he knows what your file lacks.

But you... by sharing your concerns with someone, seeking advice from another... you end up confused. Because you're not turning to the right bureau. Everyone has their own intentions. One person is here for work, another for marriage, another for studies. And you, you are here to learn, but you go and address someone who is looking for a wife. Naturally, he will tell you that you need to get married, and for that, you need X, Y, Z, etc...

Understand then... Understand that a *murīd* is of absolutely no use to another *murīd*. When you spend hours engaging in idle chatter with a fellow disciple, you should know that ultimately, you exhaust one another.

The initial intention that resided in your heart becomes vulnerable to alteration, as something else gets introduced. You might have approached the person with the intention of gaining knowledge, but they might be seeking something entirely different. They converse with you driven by their own motives, and their intent gradually begins to shape yours. Consequently, you may find yourself aspiring to emulate others rather than following your original path.

Indeed, when engaging in conversation with another person, you may inadvertently adopt their perspective, achieving their hidden goals instead of your own. Whether those goals pertain to worldly ambitions or spiritual practices such as *dhikr*, you may accomplish them, but without gaining anything beyond. Mūlay Abdul Salām ibn Mashīsh (*Quddisa Sirruh*) warns against this by saying, "Whoever leads you to the mundane (*dunya*) has certainly deceived you." A conversation between disciples often leads to worldly concerns. As for the one who believes himself superior and thinks he has understood everything, he may only guide you to *dhikr*, thereby exhausting you. But the Shaykh is different; he leads you directly to Allah ﷻ, offering you good counsel.

The Shaykh's wisdom is why he speaks openly to everyone, knowing that there is only Allah ﷻ. A disciple, on the other hand, cannot do the same. He may isolate you, needing the veils of shadows to converse, for he is filled with darkness. Unlike the Shaykh, who openly shares his wisdom, the disciple may attempt to manipulate you, inviting you to a private conversation over coffee or through messages. He claims that you'll help each other, but in reality, this interaction may confuse you and turn your heart upside down.

If the Shaykh hadn't opened your heart to understanding, it would have remained blind, stumbling in darkness without knowing where it is stepping. This underscores the importance of recognizing true guidance and the potential pitfalls of seeking wisdom from those who may lead you astray. Exercise caution and discernment in your spiritual journey, particularly in the opening of the vision of the heart (*baṣīra*), which was granted to you from the moment of the *bay`a*.

Why is it that a *murīd*, no matter who he is, cannot open this *baṣīra* for you, while we can? Because we lead people to Allah ﷻ, whereas he might lead you only to futile things, leaving your heart in turmoil. Instead of opening your heart, he may fill it with confusion, akin to filling it with sand. The same applies when you approach a *murīd*, thinking that you can open his heart. In reality, you may only be compounding his problems, obscuring his vision until he cannot see at all.

Remember, you cannot have two imams leading the same prayer. You must choose your imam wisely, as the Messenger of Allah ﷺ has said, "Your imams are your intercessors with Allah ﷻ." If you want to purify your prayer, choose the best among you as your imam. Know that the one who will intercede for you is the imam whose *hijra* was for Allah ﷻ and His Messenger ﷺ. Always evaluate why you are following someone. Is it because of material possessions, such as a 4x4 vehicle? Or because you admire their speech or general knowledge? Be mindful of your intention, for it is not necessarily the other person who is wrong, but rather your intention. If you follow someone for a specific goal or self-interest, know that you may win neither in this world nor in the Hereafter. Your intention in choosing a spiritual guide should be pure, directed towards seeking Allah ﷻ, and not influenced by superficial or worldly factors.

21.
To Achieve True Gain, Separate Yourself from the Crowd!

When the children of Sayyiduna Ya`qūb ﷺ approached him, they pleaded, **"Oh our father! Seek forgiveness for our sins; indeed, we were at fault."** He replied, **"I will seek forgiveness from my Lord: He is indeed the Most Forgiving, the Very Merciful."**[14]

Sayyiduna Ya`qūb's ﷺ prayers were efficacious because he was among those forgiven. He was one who embodied the statement of the Real: "When I love him, I become his hearing, his seeing, his hand, his foot. And when he calls on Me, I answer him."

Why does He ﷺ answer him?

Because this servant is wholly immersed in His divine proximity.

Why can't you, children of Ya`qūb ﷺ, who are in the spiritual station of the Prophets, invoke Allah ﷺ yourselves?

Because you've ensnared yourselves in the labyrinth of your ego (*nafs*), and your heedlessness (*ghafla*) has manifested as the injustice you inflicted on your brother Yūsuf ﷺ.

....

14 Sūra 12. Yūsuf, verse 97.

O *murīd*, do you grasp this?

They were guilty of injustice, so they sought the aid of the one with the greatest influence (*ta'thīr*), or the one with the most intimate connection to the Lord, to seek forgiveness on their behalf.

But what does "seek forgiveness for them" signify here?

It means to assist them in escaping the deceit of their *nafs* and the weight of the injustice they carry.

What counsel does Sayyiduna Ya`qūb ﷺ give his sons when they return to the city?

He advises: **"My sons, do not enter through one gate; instead, enter through different gates."**[15]

Why different gates?

Because when you gather, it's a catastrophe! If you gather, then you won't be eleven Prophets; rather, you'll have eleven *shaytāns* in your midst! Therefore, to avert this: separate yourselves! Separate yourselves so that the illness does not spread among you. As soon as you assemble, remember, the first time you gathered. You threw Yusuf into the well! If you repeat this, if you all enter through the same gate, you'll set a new trap for him. So, stay separate. Keep your faith's flame (*īmān*) pure within you.

We impart the same advice to the *murīd*. Avoid gathering for idle talk. The moment you assemble for chatter, you'll begin setting traps for each other. Let each of you sit in your corner, seeking the forgiveness of your Lord. Refrain from congregating for idle talk, for it will

....

15 Sūra 12. Yūsuf, verse 67.

inevitably lead you to commit the deeds of the sons of Sayyiduna Ya`qūb ﷺ. You start with two, then three. By the time you're eleven, you'll have extinguished the Pre-Eternal Sun. You won't have ignited it. You'll have indeed extinguished it!

"Father, I saw eleven stars, the Sun, and the Moon, prostrating before me."[16]

These eleven stars... they are the ones who quenched the Pre-Eternal Sun, casting Him into the well. They left Him concealed, hidden at the bottom of the well, and then later in a prison for years, until the Lord, in His preordained time, chose to bring Him back to the light.

This is the same for you. The greatest danger to a disciple arises when his peers gather around him and appoint him as their *muqaddim*. Once the *muqaddim* is appointed, he begins devising plans, which always align with the desires of the disciples' *nafs*. If he dares to express opinions that conflict with their inner desires, he risks losing his position. However, his primary goal is to maintain that position. Therefore, he acts in accordance with the wishes of the disciples to preserve the unity of the group.

That's why when Sayyiduna Mūsa ﷺ returned to his people, he spoke directly to Hārūn ﷺ, grabbing him by the beard. Because he, too, feared to speak directly to them. If he had addressed them directly, the group would have dispersed. So, what else could he do but tell them to stay there and worship the golden calf? He's

....

16 Sūra 12. Yūsuf, verse 6.

careful about his own actions, of course, he won't worship the calf. However, on the other hand, the individual who remains silent on such a grave matter... the implications are clear...

You speak of correcting the blameworthy (*al-munkar*), according to the hadith, either by force or by speech, etc... Don't you? So why don't you go to Hārūn ﷺ and sever his head for he failed to uphold this divine commandment!?

The same is for you, O *murīd*!

Change the blameworthy (*al-munkar*) in yourself, and focus on the connection with the one who will assist you with his invocations. Separate yourself from the crowd to attain your true potential because the door allows only one person to pass... not the group!

People will enter paradise in groups. But not the Divine Presence!

During the celestial ascension (*mi`rāj*), the Prophet ﷺ went from door to door, until Sayyiduna Jibrīl ﷺ told him: "If you cross, you pass, while if I cross, I burn." Meaning that only one can cross this passage. The door only admits one... not two!

And when he ﷺ met Sayyiduna Adam ﷺ, he didn't invite him, "come, let's go see Sayyiduna `Issa ﷺ in the second sky... we'll all perform *dhikr* together." No! He journeyed alone, and each remained in his own station, with his own *wird*, in the presence of the Lord, period.

So, let me ask you: why aren't you following the same path? Surely, you too harbor the aspiration for celestial ascension (*mi`rāj*)? Or perhaps your envisioned *mi`rāj* is tangled amidst the chaos of the crowd? Are you considering carrying out this divine journey as part of a caravan? If that's your plan, then stick with the caravan. But remember, your destination will only be Paradise, where you will be dwelling in a state of heedlessness (*ghafla*), immersed in bodily pleasures distracting you from gazing at the face of your Lord.

The one who enters the Divine Presence on the day of increase (*yawm al-mazīd*) does so alone. Everyone will enter individually, finding their own seat (*kursī*) to settle. And each will engage in a private conversation with the Lord. This is in *Ṣaḥīḥ al-Bukhārī*. I am not making this up, for the majority of you who are already drowning in doubts. The Lord won't address you as a group. He'll address each of you individually. To each He'll say: "Do you remember, that day when you committed this and that...?" The servant will answer "Lord! Haven't You forgiven me!?" and He'll respond "Yes, but this is for you to remember."

This tells us that He'll address each one according to his spiritual station (*maqām*), based on what they've achieved and accomplished. It's crucial, therefore, to understand that entrance into this divine presence happens individually, not collectively! Alone, because in this journey, we are advancing towards the One and Only.

Paradise, on the other hand, is different. In Paradise, there are palaces, fragrances, all conceivable fruits, and every kind of bird's meat one could desire. And there, you'll be among other people. You'll visit such and such. You'll come across a magnificent palace, ask to whom it belongs, and be told that it's the dwelling of a particular individual. And that one over there? That's someone else's dwelling. So, you'll be touring around, like you're on a sightseeing bus. And you might ask, "And what did he do to acquire such a palace?" You'll be told about specific deeds he performed. And you might think, "Ah, if only I had acted like him." Isn't this just like it is here on Earth, in the *dunya*?

Entering the presence of the Lord is a solo journey. In this place, there are no palaces, no fruits, none of that... This is the extra day, the day of Knowledge of the Lord. It's the day beyond ordinary days. And what is this day? It's the day of *jumu`a*. It's the day when everyone will be gathered (*jumi`a*) in Paradise, and the privileged ones (*ahl al-ikhtiṣāṣ*) will gain access to the presence of the Lord... alone.

22.
As the Shaykh Reveals More, the Disciple Drifts Further Away

No matter what you do, you will never fully appreciate the Shaykh. Why? Simply because you're unaware of the sanctified nature of his secret. Even if you spend your entire life with him, you will never truly know the Shaykh.

Why will you never truly know the Shaykh? Because you can only understand what he has shared with you. You can't perceive beyond what he chooses to reveal. He might have shown you a little, but to another, he might have revealed more. That person, having received more than you, fears the Shaykh. For him, sitting with the Shaykh becomes difficult.

Have you ever noticed? Who are those who sit most frequently with the Shaykh? Who jokes around with him the most?

They are the newcomers, those who have just arrived. Because they do not know the Shaykh. As such, things seem normal to them. They walk in, greet the Shaykh, start to share their stories, and notice the Shaykh's interest and openness. Upon leaving, they speak fondly of the Shaykh, describing his kindness, politeness, gentleness, and humility.

But what about the one who has received the secrets. Can he even approach the Shaykh or sit in his presence?

It's not us who forbid him, quite the contrary! It's just that the Shaykh's sanctified secrets, once revealed to him, induce fear, even terror. He is overwhelmed in the Shaykh's presence, realizing the magnitude of these secrets. He cannot approach the Shaykh.

The more the Shaykh unveils to him, the further he distances himself. This distancing isn't a sign of separation; it's a result of the reverential fear (*khashiya*) that emerges in his heart, leading him to maintain a certain distance. He becomes hesitant to speak, look, or stand beside the Shaykh.

In contrast, another might act differently, emulating the Shaykh's footsteps. How does he perceive this? He believes it's his duty to trace the Shaykh's steps exactly, placing his feet where the Shaykh does. Oblivious, he acts just like al-Sāmirī, asserting, "I follow the Shaykh's path..." Following the Shaykh's path doesn't mean literally stepping where he stepped or shadowing him!

Following the Shaykh's path means observing his journey and ensuring that you follow this trajectory throughout your life. This is what "following the Shaykh's path" truly means! His footsteps... you must never trample them. Kiss them! Show reverence to the remnants of the people of Allah ﷻ (*ahlu llah*)!

Even today, people kiss the sandals of our master al-Mustafa ﷺ! Have you ever seen anyone daring to wear them? We receive blessings (*baraka*) from the Prophet's ﷺ hair by mere sight or by touch, if one is privileged. But no one would dare to place them on their head, mixing them with their own hair! This is the true nature of *ta`dhīm*!

The *djellaba* of the Prophet ﷺ isn't meant to be worn. No! It's a source of blessing. Because it was worn by the one closest to the divine covenant (`ahd), it too embodies this closeness, and that's why we seek its blessings.

The rules of *adab* evolve with the unveiling of secrets. *Adab* is not merely a rigid daily routine or set of rules, similar to those established for interacting with kings, presidents, or ministers, with specific objectives in mind. In this context, no targeted goal or particular interest exists. Instead, adhering to proper decorum (*adab*) arises as an inherent expectation and necessity.

However, be mindful, it's not the Shaykh who imposes this expectation. Not in the slightest. It's the secrets that make *adab* obligatory for you. The unveiling of this secret within your heart is what mandates the observance of these rules.

23.
How Will the Quran Be Elevated
at the End of Times?

Indeed, the human form accepts all the attributes of divine perfection (*al-kamālāt al-ilāhiya*). But this is an extremely heavy trust (*amāna*); so heavy that Man is unable to bear it, simply because he does not like his spirit to be seized (*qabḍ*), nor his apparent form (*ṣūra*). This trust was too heavy also for the seven heavens and the seven earths. The mountains could not bear it either and ultimately it was Man who received it, thereby becoming a great wrongdoer (*dhalūm*) against himself, in what it implies to comply with the requirements of both beauty (*jamāl*) and majesty (*jalāl*).

In other words, to say that Man carries this trust is to consider that he unites all opposites. As for all other creatures, living or not, they are only inscribed in a unique perspective or dimension, lacking all others. Man is unjust (*dhalūm*) to himself for having accepted this trust which implies the union of all opposites, thereby becoming the one who provides good (*an-nāfi* `) and the one who provides harm (*aḍ-ḍārr*), the giver (*al-mu* `*tī*) and the withholder (*al-māni* `), the unjust (*al-dhalūm*) and the victim of injustice (*al-madhlūm*). All the names are in truth his own names. And Man is the most ignorant (*al-jahūl*) concerning the reality (*ḥaqīqa*) of his soul (*nafs*).

Man received the names. Had he not received them, he would not have been able to pronounce them, and he would not have been capable of praying upon the one who bore them par excellence, namely al-Mustafa ﷺ. And the Real would not then have called us: **"send prayers upon him and send [your] salutations."**[17] For it is he who truly knew how unjust we were to ourselves.

It was by receiving this trust that we were able to establish this connection, or prayer (*ṣila*), with our Prophet ﷺ. The trust is given to Man, but Man is not aware of it. Allah ﷻ says: **"Indeed, Allah ﷻ commands you to render trusts to whom they are due."**[18] One day, one of you came to me with a question. He said he wanted to return the trust to its rightful owner (*ilā ahliha*), and he wanted to know how to do it.

You, O heedless disciple, have received it, you have not assumed its burden, you have become both the wrongdoer (*al-dhālim*) and the victim of this injustice (*al-madhlūm*) that you inflict on yourself. How then would you return this trust to its rightful owner? It is very simple: you are completely incapable.

Even if you have not done the spiritual retreat (*khulwa*), even if you have not received the light, and even if you have not taken hand with me (*bay`a*): you are a human being, Muslim, born of Muslim parents. You are therefore by definition unjust (*dhālim*) and

....

17 Sūra 33. Al-Ahzab, verse 56.
18 Sūra 4. An-Nissa, verse 58.

yourself the victim of this injustice (*madhlūm*). Whoever you are, you are the one who unites this reality (*haqīqa*), you are the bearer of this burden of opposites.

Recognize, seekers of the Real, that the only true recourse you have is to lay yourself in complete prostration before the Most Gracious (*ar-Raḥmān*). One's self-imposed veils are often so confounding that discerning the rightful custodian of the divine trust (*ahl al-amāna*) becomes challenging. Yet, do not let this cloud your understanding, for it is Allah ﷻ Himself who is the deserving one (*huwa ahluh*)!

So, what does it mean to return the trust?

Returning the trust means seeking the true Reading of the divine name "Allah" and the knowledge of its different degrees. And then, it is to Allah ﷻ that you will return the trust. In this Reading, you start by throwing and abandoning yourself in His *hā'*, then you evolve on His *lām*, then on His other *lām*, then you find yourself separated (*faṣl*) and united (*waṣl*) in what will be for you a primary study of *al-alif al-muqaddar*. Then, you will return to the *hā'*, to begin the study of *lām al-qabḍ*, and you will write yourself: "I have neither form, nor breath, nor intellect, nor anything at all before the Real ﷻ! Teach me then what I do not know!"

Allah ﷻ says: **"It is He (*huwa*) who is most worthy (*ahl*) to be feared (*taqwa*), and it is He (*huwa*) who is most worthy (*ahl*) to forgive (*maghfira*)."**[19] This verse radiates indisputable clarity. O heedless disciples, every time I present you a Quranic verse, your task is to dis-

....

19 Sūra 74. Al-Muddaththir, verse 56.

sect its layers and ponder profoundly over its essence, far beyond a superficial comprehension. As you advance in your spiritual journey (*tarīq*), you'll realize that your former understanding of the Quran has undergone a metamorphosis. You'll find that what remains is a deep, thorough understanding, replacing the initial assumptions, and ensuring there's not a verse in the Quran left unexplored or unappreciated.

When I speak of "segmenting" (*qaṣ*) the Quran, this needs to be comprehended on dual fronts: Firstly, it implies dividing each verse, bringing it down into your heart, the site of spiritual manifestations, until your heart becomes a living embodiment of the Quran and its essence. Hence, the Quran will no longer be for you just a physical text to be handled with mere hands. On the other hand, for those among you who choose to negate these evident truths, I will dissect the verses for you, one after another, ultimately demonstrating that you are devoid of any substantial chapters (*sūra*).

I commenced by separating verses that referenced the light, and gradually, we are transitioning towards other verses. In undertaking this approach, we are returning everything to its Primordial Source. For we now find ourselves in the era of the end of times, a period prophesized for the ascension of the Quran. We must therefore internalize its teachings as we prepare for this pivotal moment.

But do you know who will elevate it?

A seal (*khatm*) will come, he will dissect the Quran in a total and absolute manner, and not a trace will remain. Then, the seal (*khatm*) will be seized (*qabḍ*) itself, and you will not have left even a single verse (*āya*). You will then be among those whom the Quran designates as **"like the donkey carrying scrolls."**[20]

....
20 Sūra 62. Al-Jumu`a, verse 5.

24.
"He Will Manifest to Them, Laughing"

Indeed, even in the grave, He will come to you. When He manifests, it is essential to show respect and proper decorum (*adab*), for this is His revealed ethereal presence (*hajīr*). Do not assume that the *hajīr* visiting you is an unfamiliar being whom you'll encounter for the first time in the grave. Instead, the visitor will surely be one you already know.

When you sit for an examination, it is conducted by the one who taught you. If you have been studying mathematics, you wouldn't seek a philosophy professor to administer your test. Scientists take their exams with scientists, and philosophers with philosophers. You are learning the esoteric science (*al-ʿilm al-ladunī*). So, present your knowledge, and let me give you your examination! Or are you hoping that someone else will come to test you!?

Do you engage in *dhikr* with the hope that al-Khidr will be your ultimate examiner?

No! al-Khidr ﷺ came to test Mūsa ﷺ. You have to deal with your own Shaykh!

If you don't understand this here and now... you will have to face it on the day of your examination. If you don't grasp the lesson in the classroom, it will come back to you on the day of the test, O heedless disciple!

The hadith says: "The Lord manifests Himself [on the Day of Judgment] to the worshippers of fire through their fire", it signifies that the very fire they worshipped, the fire that served as their manifestation (*hajīr*) in this world, it is this fire that will test them on the Last Day. For the worshippers of `Uzayr ﷺ, He will manifest Himself in `Uzayr ﷺ. He will manifest Himself through whatever they worshipped other than Allah ﷻ. This will continue until only the believers remain.

Regarding those who lived according to the doctrine of **"Nothing is like His example (*laysa kamithlihi shay'*)"**[21] the hadith tells us that, "He will manifest Himself to them, laughing (*wa huwa yadḥak*)".

Why will He laugh? Will there be a comedy show to prompt laughter!?

Certainly not!

When you hear "*wa huwa yadḥak*," you should understand that you will weep. For the Lord embodies opposites. He makes people laugh and cry. And remember, when He laughs, you will weep. He will ask: "What are you waiting for?", and the response will be: "We are waiting for our Lord!" The Lord questions what you are waiting for, and you respond that you are waiting for your Lord! This is where your spiritual recognition (*ma`rifa*) falters. The Lord will evaluate you based on your answer.

....

21 Sūra 42. Ash-Shūra, verse 11.

Let us tread carefully, for we are delving into the depths of *Ṣaḥīḥ al-Bukhāri*. Do not dare to dismiss this as mere tales or inauthentic narrations. This is *Ṣaḥīḥ*, affirmed by al-Bukhāri himself, upon whom may Allah ﷻ bestow His pleasure. Remember, the esteemed al-Bukhāri would not accept a hadith from one who deceived his very horse by simulating a feed. Such was his commitment to truth and integrity. So, when we speak of *Ṣaḥīḥ al-Bukhāri*, let it be with the profound reverence it rightfully commands.

On that momentous day, He will address those believers enveloped in ignorance, asking: "Do you carry with you a sign from Him that might aid you in recognizing His presence?" On that day, the flimsy veils of this world will be lifted.

You won't be able to hide behind the self-congratulatory claims and pseudo-intellectual bravado you parade in this *dunya*, boasting in front of fellow Muslims, "But I was told by others... and then I read in books that..." No! When that day dawns, the question will pierce your soul: Do you hold anything tangible, anything real, to truly recognize your Lord? Step forward and unveil what you genuinely possess!

So what will you be able to present at that moment? Can you pull out your Islamic studies handouts? Or reach into your school bag and pull out *Ṣaḥīḥ al-Bukhāri* and *Muslim*?

No! On that momentous day, you will have to open your heart, and bring forth the book that resides within it!

When He will ask you: "Do you have from Him a sign..." What will be your sign?

It is the light of Allah ﷻ!

On that moment, the light of Allah ﷻ will appear to every Muslim. All Muslims, without exception, who remain waiting will witness the light of Allah ﷻ on that Day. Including the hypocrites!

Why the hypocrites too?

Because they didn't believe in it while they were alive. Therefore, the Lord will reveal it to them, prompting their belief. They will see it! Then, Allah ﷻ will extinguish their light, leaving it only for the true Muslims. Then, Muslims will traverse the *ṣirāt* (bridge). The believers will be divided into two groups: the first group's faces (*wujūh*) -and on that day, the face of a believer is his façade that reflects what is in his heart- will shine like the moon at its fullest. This signifies those who perceive the light of Allah ﷻ as a full moon, they are the people of the first group, those who will traverse the *ṣirāt* with the speed of lightning. And hell will implore them: "O believer, cross quickly! for your light extinguishes my fire."

Your light... not you! Hell doesn't fear you. You are insignificant!

Then, the second group to cross are those who see a light akin to the brightest star in the sky. That is, the star that you receive at the *bay`a* (initiatory pledge).

Thus, don't you recognize that, on that day, the Lord will offer you the same *bay`a*? The same *bay`a* that you took while alive! Understand this very well heedless disciple. On the Last Day, the Lord will manifest Himself to you, laughing, and He will lift the veils and enable you to see the light. That is, Allah ﷻ will project His light into your heart and some will perceive it as a full moon, while others will see it as the brightest star in the sky. Isn't this the same scenario repeating itself!?

The people of the first group will cross "at the speed of lightning." That is, space will be bent for them. And you, don't you say that you too journey in the heavens during your *dhikr* at an extraordinary speed. You say you see worlds and galaxies. Isn't space being bent for you as well!? You barely notice the darkness anymore since you are rushing through in what you call cosmic tunnels, tubes, or concentric waves of light. Aren't you moving at an extraordinary speed then!? Ask those to whom the light of the Lord reveals itself! These individuals will cross, free of judgement! And why free of judgement? Because in this world, they were among those who held themselves accountable. They held themselves accountable before they were called to account. The deeds they performed here are from the past. They won't face the same scrutiny in the afterlife. They've already been through that process, so for them, everything is in place.

As for the others, those who didn't hold themselves accountable in this life, their judgement awaits in the afterlife. So, how will they be judged?

They will attempt to cross the *ṣirāṭ*[22], and as they step on it... Allah ﷻ will extinguish their light. Because they did not trust in the light of the Lord! Instead, they trusted their own deeds, their memorization of *Ṣaḥīḥ al-Bukhārī*

....

22 In Islamic eschatology, "aṣ-Ṣirāṭ" refers to the thin bridge that souls must cross on the Day of Judgment.

and *Muslim*. They memorized the Quran, **"like a donkey carrying volumes."**[23] They even memorized its different readings, **"Thus do We insert it into the hearts of the criminals."**[24]

Then, hooks will appear, ensnaring people's feet. What are these hooks? These represent all the distractions you harbor within. These distractions are present in your prayers, in your charitable acts, and in your fasting; they are a product of your pride, vanity, and jealousy. An individual will attempt to cross the bridge, only to be snagged by these distractions, these hooks. However, it's not definitive that they will inevitably fall, nor is it guaranteed that they will successfully cross; their destiny lies in Allah's ﷻ hands. The fate of these Muslims is uncertain.

The only certainty lies in the fate of the first and second group, who will traverse the bridge without judgment. As for the others, it is in Allah's ﷻ hands. If He wills, He will save them from the fire. If He decides otherwise, He will call them to account for their deeds. Then, they may fall into the fire.

This is the true understanding of "He will appear to them, laughing (*wa huwa yadḥak*)." On earth, they made a mockery of Him and in the afterlife, it is He who will have the last laugh. They distorted the interpretations of the Quran here, refusing to accept the divine commands and verses as they are and, in the afterlife, the Lord will call them to account.

....

23 Sūra 62. Al-Jumu'ah, verse 5.
24 Sūra 15. Al-Hijr, verse 12.

25.
**"O Lord, Grant Me a Kingdom that Shall
not Befit Anyone After Me!"**

The one who provides refreshment, the cupbearer (*al-sāqī*), is none other than the drinker (*al-shārib*) himself. The wine rises from within you, towards you, intoxicating you with your own essence. Only the name remains while you embody its profound and eternal significance.

But how could you be the profound meaning of the name?

If you ponder over the name in its written form (*mastūr*), you ought to savor the truth of reading the *hā'* through its ten degrees. In this process, you will find yourself divested of your body, your attributes, your visible form, and your name until finally, your spirit can be seized (*qabḍ*) in an absolute and permanent manner, leaving no trace of yourself behind. And if no trace of you remains, your movements become unrestricted (*itlāq*), and your characteristics adopt celestial qualities. You then transform into a luminous oblivion (`*amā'*), and from this luminous oblivion, the absolute essence of the name Allah ﷻ emerges. This transformation happens as your ultimate goal was to revert to the reality of Divine Command (*al-ḥaqīqa al-amriyya*), and consequently to the knowledge of lordship (*ma`rifat al-rubūbuyya*).

When this name eventually splits (*inshaqqa*), where will you find yourself?

You will find yourself in this boundary, this absolute luminous oblivion (`*amā*'), as if on the isthmus of this *lām al-qabḍ*. From this spiritual station, Prophet Sulaymān ﷺ stated: **"Grant me a kingdom (*mulk*) that is unfit for anyone after me."**[25] This implies that he sought the ultimate essence (*al-dhāt al-`aliyya*), and didn't merely stick to the numerous names and attributes. Thus, everything turned and referred back to him, and he saw absolutely nothing else, neither before him nor after him.

In essence, when an individual reaches this sacred spiritual dimension (*ḥaḍra aqdasiyya*), they no longer see or consider the form of another. All that remains is a complete and definitive dissolution in the presence of the Ultimate Truth and Reality. There is neither a before nor an after, for the individual has then lost the concept of time, his existence, and anything that could hint at a pronoun. There are no more pronouns or forms for him. Rather, he only has *huwa*, which means "he," as **"there is nothing like unto him,"**[26] Unique, Exclusive, Singular, the only one to be considered.

The beholder of this spiritual state no longer sees anyone else but himself, both in the past and the future. He embodies both the past and future existence. To

....

25 Sūra 38. Sad, verse 35.
26 Sūra 42. Ash-Shūra, verse 11.

him, eternity and pre-eternity are indistinguishable, signifying total freedom: **"This is Our bestowal. So, give or withhold as you wish without account."**[27] Among the abilities within his realm is commanding the wind. As soon as he experienced annihilation (*fanā'*), never to return from it, he became akin to the water flowing through everything, even circulating in the air, in objects, devoid of color or shape.

A peculiar characteristic of his realm includes the feat of visiting 100 wives in one night, an act humanly unattainable. According to Abu Hurayra ﷺ: "Sulaymān عليه السلام son of Dāwud عليه السلام said: 'I will visit a hundred women tonight, each of whom will give birth to a boy who will fight in the way of Allah ﷻ.' An angel told him: 'Say: Inshā'Allah ﷻ (if Allah ﷻ wills)!' But he did not say it. He indeed visited these women, but only one of them gave birth to a half-man." This hadith, reported by *al-Bukhāri* is authentic and irrefutable. Here, we have a man, a human being, visiting a hundred women in a single night. Even if one imagines the Lord granting the physical prowess for such an act, how could this feat be achieved within the confines of a single day? Neither twelve nor twenty-four hours would suffice. It requires more hours than known.

Know, disciple, that when you attain this state of spiritual elevation, you experience the rapid folding (*al-tayy*) of time and space. This ability (*qudra*) originates from the Real and manifests in one of His creatures whom He has specifically prepared and shaped for this purpose.

....

27 Sūra 38. Ṣad, verse 39.

Once an individual is wholly annihilated, with no trace of existence, they indeed possess the capacity to transcend time and space, achieving what those confined by the constraints of spatial directions and the shackles of nonexistence cannot.

26.
Looking Behind Oneself During Prayer

The letter *lām* signifies the potential of adopting certain character traits (*khuluq*), aligning oneself with the nature of *ar-Raḥmān*. This alignment does not mean one has fully reached the pinnacle of spiritual realization, represented by the *alif*, but rather that one has taken a significant step towards it. This progression can be thought of as having achieved an approximation or embodiment of the form the *lām* could take. Hence, we can assert that the person in question possesses the *lām*, but not yet the *alif*.

Why?

Simply because the *lām* is curved. The letter *lām* (ل), when pronounced, is articulated with a *lām* followed by a *mīm* (م). The numerical value of *lām* is 30, and that of *mīm* is 40, equating to the 70 from: "Between the Real and creation there are seventy veils of light and darkness." In actuality, this denotes seventy veils of light and seventy veils of darkness, representing the two *lāms*. These two *lāms* are nothing more than the two *lāms* found in the *lām al-qabḍ*.

The *lām al-qabḍ* is so named because it involves a process of seizing (*qabḍ*) the seeker's spiritual essence.

When your spiritual essence is seized, its dark aspect is entirely obliterated, transforming you into light.

And who achieves this degree?

Naturally, it is al-Mustafa ﷺ, by virtue of the hadith *qudsī*: "I seized (*qabaḍtu*) a handful (*qabḍatan*) of My light and said to it: 'Be Muhammad!'" Or as the verse describes: **"an illuminating lamp."**[28] Therefore, if you ascend to embody the character of al-Mustafa ﷺ, it's as if you, in turn, become a small luminous lamp. If you were to describe al-Mustafa ﷺ, you could say he is the entirety of the universe. He then adorns this universe: "My companions are like the stars: follow any one of them, and you will be guided rightly." If you find what I say unsatisfactory, then feel free to dismiss the hadith of al-Mustafa ﷺ.

Therefore, as a seeker, you must reserve seventy veils of light for al-Mustafa ﷺ. And regarding yourself, you must encapsulate within your own ego (*nafs*) the seventy veils of darkness. Understand that if you recognize yourself as a shadowed being and recognize al-Mustafa ﷺ as the radiant essence, you stand as the shadow of al-Mustafa ﷺ. You have then truly fulfilled the command: "Pray as you have seen me pray."

Sayyiduna al-Mustafa ﷺ proclaims: "Prayer is light, and fasting is radiance." And he ﷺ also declared: "Line up correctly and huddle close, for I see you behind me just as I see you in front of me."

What does this signify?

....

28   Sūra 33. Al-Ahzab, verse 46.

Prayer is light and al-Mustafa ﷺ perceived behind him implies that he ﷺ became **"light upon light. Allah ﷻ guides to His light whom He wills."**[29] Or to put it in simpler terms, prayer and al-Mustafa ﷺ are one and the same.

Therefore, you can deduce that, during your prayer, it's as if you exist as a shadow of the Prophet ﷺ. This explains why your prayer is only valid to the extent that you acknowledge the Prophet ﷺ as your imam. However, if you conceive yourself as the imam leading this prayer then you commit *shirk* with his light, asserting that it's yours and not his.

The Messenger of Allah ﷺ succinctly summarized all this in one phrase: "My companions..." By this, he meant those who have truly lived with their bodies alongside his, those who accompanied him both physically and spiritually, "...are like the stars." It's as if he's saying: "I am their Sun, and they are my stars." In essence, they are the shadows or reflections of his light. This is what the *lām al-qabḍ* represents.

Hence, from this discourse, you should discern that your commitment to the Shaykh will only be valid to the extent that your shadow has been wholly and absolutely seized.

But when is the shadow seized? Or to frame the question differently: when does the shadow of things completely vanish?

According to the laws of science, it happens when the sun is precisely overhead. In other words, if al-Mustafa ﷺ

....

29   Sūra 24. An-Nur, verse 35.

appears to you as *an-nuqta ash-shādhdha*, the point above the *alif* and if you truly regard him in that light, then the shadow of your being disappears and is engulfed by his radiance. If his light entirely envelops you, then darkness no longer exists. And when the darkness disappears, who truly loses their existence? Evidently, it is the seeker who has achieved this degree of detachment (*tajarrud*). If he has fully eliminated all innate darkness, he then gains the capability to see both what's behind and ahead of him. Nonetheless, he will maintain decorum (*adab*) and won't declare, "I see behind me!" Instead, he will articulate, "Through the eyes of the Prophet ﷺ, I see behind me."

27.
What Is the Only Islamic Science Exempt from Dissent?

Zayd ibn Arqam ﷺ reported that the Messenger of Allah ﷺ said, "I entrust to you that which, if you hold firmly onto, will shield you from deviation after me. Understand that one of these is more significant than the other: the Book of Allah ﷻ, a rope extended from the sky to the earth, and the elite of my progeny (`*itratī ahli baytī*). They shall remain inseparable until they reunite with me at the Pool."

`*Itratī ahli baytī* refers to the quintessence of *ahl al-bayt*. It's not about any individual of *ahl al-bayt*. We are rather discussing the `*itra*!

These are the two things to which you must adhere. Thus, didn't the Messenger of Allah ﷺ provide a concrete example?

He likened the Quran to a rope... to help you perceive it as more than a physical book. The Prophet ﷺ depicted it as a rope, encouraging you to envision it in this way. Remember! These are the words of the Prophet ﷺ, and he doesn't speak out of mere passion. Whether you regard my words as significant is irrelevant. But here, we're dealing with the description provided by the Prophet ﷺ himself! Leave aside your ego, your references, your studies, and your intellect. Just please don't interfere with or corrupt the Prophetic words!

When we say rope, we mean a rope! Don't look for alternative interpretations! This is not a description given by a scholar, a professor, a doctor, or anyone else. Therefore, you can't bring your own interpretation. Allah ﷻ indeed says: **"He does not speak out of passion: it is indeed a revelation revealed to him."**[30]

It's a revelation (*waḥiy*), so when he tells you it's a rope, it's a rope. And when he mentions `itra*, he means `itra*. Period. He advises you to cling to these two elements not merely to know them! There is a significant difference between the two terms. "Hold firmly onto" (*tamassak*) is not the same as "get to know" (*ta`arraf*)! *Tamassak* implies holding tightly to this rope and this `itra*.

But what do we have today?

Today, we have an abundance of books. We no longer have a single book, we have many!

Why do we have a multitude of books?

Simply because interpretations vary. There is not just one single interpretation for everything. Whether it's for the exegesis of the Quran, for *fiqh*, or any other discipline, all are marked by disagreement. In the *Mālikī* madhhab, for instance, you will find a sea of juridical opinions (*ijtihādāt*). The same is true for all other schools of jurisprudence. As a result, you may find it hard to know where to turn.

....

30 Sūra 53. An-Najm, verses 3-4.

However, during the time of the Messenger of Allah ﷺ, these divergences did not exist. The watchword was: "Pray as you have seen me pray." It was as simple as that! You mirrored the Prophet's ﷺ actions. If you understood why, excellent, and if you didn't, you still performed the actions, until understanding came. There were no statements like "so-and-so said" or "so-and-so thinks that."

Thus, understand disciple that when the Messenger of Allah ﷺ tells you he left behind two things, it is your duty to cling to them, with the ultimate goal being to reach the Lord through them. These are two explicit, definite, and precise elements, two elements not subject to disagreement.

Now, I need you to point to a discipline, just one discipline since the advent of the Messenger of Allah ﷺ, that harbors no dissent. Upon careful examination, you'll find it's only Sufism. The people of Allah ﷻ all share the same teachings, the same words. Read all the books of the people of Allah ﷻ. Bring me just one of their books, and say: "Sidi Shaykh, you claim this, yet in this book, the author says otherwise." I haven't read the books of Sufism, but I still challenge you to find a single statement that contradicts what I teach. The reason for this is that the source is unique. For the people of Sufism, the Book is unique, and the `itra is unique. No disagreement can arise, regardless of time and location.

However, remember that I am referring to genuine Sufism (*taṣawwuf*). I'm not alluding to... well, you know what I mean. In this context, we delve into authentic Sufism. We address the essence of the Sufi discipline. There's a singular focus, a unified discourse. Whether it's al-Jīlī, ibn Arabi, Abdul Qādir al-Jīlānī, or any other Shaykh, regardless of their origin or era, their message is consistent. When they touch upon the *'itra* of *ahl al-bayt*, their perspective stands distinct. There's complete harmony!

Now consider the other disciplines, even the Quran! The Quran could be recited according to one reading or another, narrated by one person or another. Some recitations are considered authentic, others not...

All these disagreements among sects and groups stem from an outward intent to diminish the original strength and vitality of the religion among the members of the Muslim community. There seems to be a reluctance to allow the Water to remain absolute Water (*mā' mutlaq*), leading to the addition of other elements... Even in *fiqh*, you'll see that one can perform ablutions with rainwater as well as well water. But yet, they are very different!

Allah ﷻ says: **"And We have sent down blessed water from the sky, by which We brought forth gardens and grain every harvester reaps, and tall palm-trees, with arranged clusters, a provision for the servants, and We gave life thereby to a dead land. Thus, is the resurrection."**[31]

The water that descends from the sky is alive and life-giving. It differs greatly from other waters. This water is a stretched rope. This water is akin to the Quran. Because the Quran too was sent down from heaven to earth, right?

....

31 Sūra 50. Al-Qaf, verses 9-11.

This descending water is the Quran. For when the Quran descended, it descended with it. And likewise, when water descends from the sky, the Quran descends with it. The Quran is continuously descending, even to this day. You might ask, how so?

Well, consider this: **"Ar-Raḥmān taught the Quran."**[32] The Quran, like a stretched rope, descends into a receptacle. And what is this receptacle? It is a vessel that receives this life-giving water. However, it is not just any vessel; it's made from clay. The element that is revived by the descent of water from the sky is the earth. And this earthen vessel, this vessel made from clay, symbolizes mankind itself: **"He created man from a clay like pottery."**[33] This clay vessel receives the descending water, the Quran. And, hence, the essence of man is rejuvenated by the Quran, just as the earth is rejuvenated by the water descending from the sky.

Therefore, when you are urged to hold firmly onto the Quran and the `itra`, it is more than just following written words or obeying a set of rules. It is about internalizing the essence of the teachings, imbibing the spirit of the Quran, and embodying the virtues of the `itra`. This spiritual rejuvenation that comes from the continued descent of the Quran into the vessel of your heart forms the basis of Sufism.

In other fields of study, you may find contradictions and divergences, but not in Sufism. Its source is singular, its message is uniform, and its path is clear. This

....

32 Sūra 55. Ar-Rahman, verses 1.
33 Sūra 55. Ar-Rahman, verses 14.

unity in teaching, the lack of dissent, is what distinguishes Sufism from other disciplines. The teachings of Sufism remain the same, regardless of the time, location, or the person conveying them. This is the only Islamic science that remains untouched by disagreement and divergence.

The aforementioned verse, **"Ar-Raḥmān taught the Quran,"** illustrates the continuous and ongoing revelation of the Quran. It is not a static text, but a dynamic, living teaching that continuously descends onto those who open their hearts to receive it. This is the essence of Sufism, a practice and discipline that revolves around the constant, vibrant, and living interaction with the Quran and its luminous essence. And in holding on to the `*itra*, one aligns themselves with the virtuous path of the Prophet's ﷺ household, integrating their principles and values into daily life. This spiritual journey transcends mere intellectual understanding, it is about embodying and living these teachings.

Therefore, our approach to the prophetic injunction of holding tightly to the Quran and the `*itra* is not merely about literalism or blind obedience, as our detractors falsely accuse us. Instead, it emphasizes the transformative power these two forces can exert on a receptive heart. It is about spiritual transformation, rejuvenation, and alignment with the divine will. And this is the core of Sufism—a journey towards the divine, guided by the continued descent of the Quran and the virtuous path of the `*itra*.

28.
What You Witness During Your *Bay`a* Reveals the Value of Your Past Life

When the Shaykh chooses to assist you during the transmission of the light, he does so within the confines of your intellect. He instructs you, "Close your eyes... forget your wife, your job, your children... cleanse yourself, face the *qibla*..." Yet, you persist, wringing your heart over past actions when, in truth, everything you did in the past was destined to bring you to this *Walī*.

As the verse goes, **"Allah is the *Walī* of those who have faith (īmān)..."**, not merely of those who practice Islam. It extends to those who have nurtured the various aspects of *īmān*. Why have they done so? To reach the *Walī*, who can guide them from darkness into light. They are believers (*mu'minīn*), they have faith, but they are in darkness.

Your value, as estimated by the *Walī*, is based on all that you have done for Allah ﷻ, all the *dhikr*, all the worship you've performed, and the efforts you've made to seek divine knowledge. The *Walī's* estimation considers all that you've gone through to reach him. He then allows you to see this glimmer (*lamḥa*), which represents the value of everything you've accomplished since your birth. Don't expect more than this. You sought the Shaykh to reveal your life's worth, and he showed it to you.

But this is not a secret. The secret of sainthood (*wilāya*) is more profound. Seeing the light doesn't mean that Allah ﷻ has granted you the great spiritual opening (*fatḥ*), or that you've uncovered the secrets of *wilāya*. No! You've merely seen your portion and contemplated it in the mirror of *wilāya*.

Ever since you turned seven years old, the age at which your actions began to be documented, you can now see their true worth. But understand, I'm not merely expressing some sort of feelings or beliefs! The verse clearly states: **"Allah is the *Walī* (*allahu walī*) of those who have faith: He brings them from darknesses into the Light."**[34] Delve into its interpretation, explore Sufi books, and grasp the meaning of *"Allahu Walī"*!

Linguistically, it implies that Allah ﷻ sent His *Walī* to the believers (*mu'minīn*) to guide them from their self-inflicted darknesses to the divine light. They were lost, misguided, engulfed by the lower world (*dunya*) and their egos (*nafs*). However, they carried out virtuous deeds. Their good deeds offset their bad ones. They accumulated these actions, some over 40 years, others over 20 years, each according to their divine predestination, until finally meeting the *Walī*. Others, the deprived ones (*maḥrūmīn*), may never meet him in their lifetime. Those who never meet the *Walī* will face the same process, but in the afterlife. Their good and

....

34 Sūra 2. Al-Baqarah, verse 257.

bad actions will be evaluated; their sins erased by good deeds. They'll see what remains. If there's an atom left, they'll receive the reward (*ajr*). As for those who encounter the *Walī* and perceive an atom, this atom enables them to behold the Face of the Lord. That is to say, the first group attains a reward (*ajr*), whereas the second—those blessed enough to meet the *Walī* in their lifetime—acquire spiritual knowledge (*ma`rifa*).

This is termed as *lamḥa*. *Lamḥa* isn't about size, be it small or large. We use the term *lamḥa* because of its swift unveiling to the disciple. As for its size, the hadith clearly states: "It increases and decreases based on virtuous deeds." This hadith is unequivocal. There's no need for further examination.

Your virtuous deeds too have varied consistently. When you present these virtuous deeds to the *Walī*, and he then reveals the *lamḥa* to you, what do you do? You painstakingly recount everything you've achieved. But what happens next? When you disclose all this, asking in return for secrets based on your "virtuous" deeds, it's as if you're requesting judgment and reward based on your actions.

At that juncture, the *Walī* removes this *lamḥa*. Why? Simply because the *lamḥa* supersedes all deeds. It's the *lamḥa* that elevates deeds, not the deeds that amplify the *lamḥa*. You might think that deeds produce the *lamḥa*. As a result, the *Walī* takes it away from you, plunging you into darkness. Now, bow down and humble your ego by putting your face in the sand...

29.

How Can You Calm Your Heart When You Are Unable to Gather the Strength to Practice *Dhikr* to Fill Your Heart with Light?

When Allah ﷻ imposed prayer, He first decreed 50. But why 50? A single *rak`a* or a single invocation could suffice: **"Therein they will find what they desire: '*Salām*,' a word from a Very Merciful Lord."**[35] Why then 50 daily prayers?

It's to ensure the *nāṣiya* (the spiritual forelock) remains perpetually prostrated on the earth. This prevents the *nāṣiya* from conjuring illusions and creating images mistaken for the *ḥaqīqa*, the ultimate truth. Initially, Allah ﷻ mandated fifty prayers to suppress these illusions.

However, when the Prophet Muhammad ﷺ descended to meet Prophet Mūsa عليه السلام, things changed. The 50 prayers were initially obligatory at the stage of "You are as You described Yourself," representing the ultimate and exhaustive light. But when the Messenger of Allah ﷺ descended to the sixth heaven, to Sayyiduna Mūsa عليه السلام— that is, in this path that we took the trouble to make you understand that it was only illusions—what did the

....

35   Sūra 50. Qaf, verse 35.

143

latter ﷺ tell him? Prophet Mūsa ﷺ said the *umma* wouldn't bear fifty prayers. Based on his experience with his own people, even two prayers were a challenge, so fifty would be insurmountable. He suggested Prophet Muhammad ﷺ to go back to the Real, and ask for a reduction. Following this, the Prophet ﷺ returned to the Real, and the number of prayers was decreased until there were only five left. He felt shy to ask for any further reduction. However, the value of these five prayers remained equivalent to fifty. This way, the *nāṣiya* receives the tranquilizing dose from five prayers as it would from fifty.

When you dig into the earth where you prostrate yourself, what do you find? There's no treasure but Gog and Magog, and hellfire. Remember, mercy exists on the earth's surface, not beneath. That's why we bury the dead just deep enough to be covered because mercy lies at the surface. Beneath, there's only death, fire, hell, and *Iblīs*.

Where do you prostrate again? On the surface of the earth, right?! When you prostrate, all illusions accumulated by the *nāṣiya* are released and they burn in the earth's core. At this moment, in exchange, the Lord grants His proximity because during prostration the servant is closest to his Lord.[36] Your *nāṣiya*, full of illusions and errors, is purged hence like a magnet pulling out all the filth you accumulated.

....

36 Prophet Muhammad ﷺ said in the hadith reported in *Ṣaḥīḥ Muslim*: "The time when the servant is closest to his Lord is when he is prostrating."

What about the heart, will it prostrate?

No, the heart remains elevated above the earth because it is not subjected to illusions. The parts of your body that interact with illusions: the feet, the hands, the forehead, they prostrate. The forehead, in particular, often perceives itself as the sovereign. However, the true sovereign is the heart. Allah ﷻ indeed says: **"except for one who comes to Allah with a sound heart."**[37] What hinders the heart from being sound (*salīm*)? It's the *nāṣiya*.

Therefore, we must instruct the *nāṣiya* in two duties. The first one is *jihād*. What does this *jihād* (struggle) involve? Let me tell you the bare minimum. If I'm incapable of doing *dhikr*, if I cannot attain a state where my heart is illuminated with Allah's ﷻ light... When I engage in my supererogatory prayers, I commit to a prostration lasting half an hour. Upon rising, I immediately return to another prostration of the same length. I resolutely declare that my *nāṣiya* will remain there. As soon as I hear its whispers... when it conveys to me that it's at peace, empty, with nothing lingering... I respond with a firm "no," insisting it remains in its position.

During this prostration, I continue as long as thoughts emerge in my mind. However, remember, this is only for supererogatory prayer, not obligatory ones. You don't want to keep everyone waiting behind you. It's you who needs it, with a mind filled to the brim, much like a large gourd! Understand that some people have clear minds, driven purely by their love for Allah ﷻ. For them,

....

37 Sūra 26. Ash-Shu'ara, verse 89.

a brief prostration and merely saying "*subḥāna rabbia al-a`lā*" is enough. Therefore, adopt this practice during voluntary prayers. Empty yourself completely and allow the magnet to draw out everything it can. Fire consumes fire. Darkness engulfs darkness.

Continue this until tranquility fills your heart, realizing that indeed, the Lord is near to you. When you achieve this state, rise and perceive the realization of: "Here you are: you and your Lord (*hā 'anta wa rabbuk*)." Then, declare: "You are as You have described Yourself." Through this, your heart becomes sound (*salīm*), filled with tranquility and peace, all derived from the love of the Lord.

This is the task you struggle to perform, even though it's fundamentally quite straightforward...

30.

The Awakened Visions (*mushāhadāt*) of Images and Forms Do not Align with the Quest for *Ḥaqīqa*

The issue lies in our attachment to cultural norms (*al-ʿurf*) overshadowing our love for religion. In other words, we are creatures of habit. Ponder on this: Why did people worship idols besides Allah ﷻ? It's because idol worship was ingrained in them. They inherited it from their ancestors. From the moment they were born, they witnessed their families cherishing these idols. Therefore, it's not an overnight process to shift one's worship to an "invisible" ultimate truth—to worship Allah ﷻ without seeing Him.

Consider the followers of Sayyiduna Mūsa عليه السلام: even with their knowledge of this ultimate truth, the apparent forms remained deeply rooted in their hearts. When a calf was presented to them and it bellowed in their presence, they immediately began to worship it. Why? Because apparent forms have a profound effect on people. In simpler terms, illusions influence illusions. This illusion that resides in your *nāṣiya* greatly affects you.

But what does your *nāṣiya* contain?

Your *nāṣiya* is a repository of illusions, a collection of all the illusions since the beginning of creation. You, as an individual, are non-existent. It's your *nāṣiya* that convinces you otherwise at every moment. It's the one convincing you of the independent existence of the earth and the sky. Know, disciple, that you, by yourself, do not exist. The *nāṣiya*, however, imposes its reality onto you, making you believe otherwise.

So, how can you regain control over it?

Firstly, the divine light needs to illuminate your heart. This light of your heart must unify with the light of hearing, sight, and speech. Once this happens, the *nāṣiya* will no longer affect you. If your hearing, sight, and speech are bathed in light, its influence on you will wane.

Practically, what must you do?

You have to resist its influence: **"No, do not obey it, but prostrate and draw nearer."**[38]

If you cannot prostrate yourself perpetually in the light, then at least, prostrate yourself on the ground. Stay in prostration so that your darkness drains away, and all these base thoughts leave you and vanish into the earth. However, you want to unify your heart with your *nāṣiya*. You let doubt creep in, neglect the *subḥa*, and then you question the value of the Tariqa...

Why?

Because this Tariqa aims to strip away your illusions, while your *nāṣiya* clings to them. Your *nāṣiya* thrives on these illusions. This is its mode of existence. Its exis-

....

38   Sūra 96. Al-ʿAlaq, verses 19

tence culminates in this illusory "I". That's why it's located at the highest point of your head.

The *nāṣiya* never ceases to vie for control, to dominate. It always considers itself superior. And in its arrogance, it warns you: "Don't be fooled! That person who wants to convince you that you are just an illusion, and that the entire universe is but a mirage, is lying to you and fooling you. No, the universe is not a mirage! What he is saying is deception and sorcery!"

With such a mindset, please tell me what doesn't fall under the categories of deception and sorcery?

"No! remain faithful to the *qibla*, and pray."

Why does it urge you to remain faithful to the *qibla* and pray?

Simply because it understands you. It recognizes that you are among those who worship the *Ka`ba*, not the Lord of the *Ka`ba*. Thus, it embellishes this belief in your heart, transforming it into an idol. It encourages you to concentrate on this, for it prefers this over you discovering the absolute truth. Because, if you recognized the absolute truth, who then could dominate and subjugate you?

When you engage in *dhikr*, your heart becomes luminous; light radiates within you. However, the *nāṣiya* intervenes, introducing images (*al-ṣuwar*) into your mind. Understand, disciple, that you are gazing upon the light of Allah ﷻ. Through this divine light, you begin your ascent. The light of the *alif al-muqaddar* reaches you at the first sphere of the earth, and through it, you climb along this rope extending from the heavens.[39]

What does the *nāṣiya* do when you start journeying towards the second heaven with the light of the *wilāya*?

While you are aiming for the second heaven, your *nāṣiya* distracts you with galaxies. Saturn, Uranus, the Milky Way, etc... Instead of contemplating the creation of the heavens and the earth, you become consumed with the images of the heavens and the earth. Here, you are not seeking the Creator of these images but becoming lost in the images themselves.

However, you claim: "I am taking off, I am leaving the earth, I am leaving the sphere!"

Awaken your intellect!

What will emerge before you after this? What will you behold?

You'll see the moon. Yet, seeing the moon doesn't imply you've arrived at your destination... Learn from those who genuinely sought the truth: **"When he saw the moon rising, he said, 'This is my Lord!'"**[40] Here, he issued a reminder to his *nāṣiya*. He stated: "I seek my Lord! And if anything stands in the way of my pursuit of divine lordship (*rubūbiyya*), then: **'I do not love**

....

39 This refers to the hadith: "I entrust to you that which, if you hold firmly onto, will shield you from deviation after me. Understand that one of these is more significant than the other: the Book of Allah ﷻ, a rope extended from the sky to the earth, and the elite of my progeny (`*itratī ahli baytī*). They shall remain inseparable until they reunite with me at the Pool. Therefore, consider how you will honor me through these two entities."

40 Sūra 6. Al-An'am, verse 77.

those that set.[41] My sole aim is the knowledge of "There you are, you and your Lord (*hā' anta wa rabbuk*)."

But you, no. You stay fixated with the moon. You measure its size, remark on its apparent vastness. You boast to other disciples, "This moon I see is very, very large..." The *nāṣiya* then diverts your attention to something even grander. Following that, you truly perceive something larger. And so, it persists with its other deceptions... Do you understand?

You, let me tell you what you are doing. You're wandering. You're engrossed in the display as if engrossed in a movie. But when will you begin seeking the Lord of these heavens and this earth?! Rather than diverting your gaze from the earth and ascending towards the primary truth (*ḥaqīqa*), the light of the heavens and the earth, you become lost within the heavens. Considering there are 500 years between each heaven, as per the hadith... when will you finish this voyage? 500 years to reach the second heaven, then another 500 for the third, and another 500 after that...

Your *nāṣiya*, of course, revels in this. Tomorrow, when you sit with those like you, you'll say: "I, I saw the first heaven... Unbelievable, right?! I saw also the Milky Way... And what about you?"

"I, I saw a creature... *subḥānAllah* , I had never seen anything like it."

"I, I saw this..."

"I, I saw that..."

No!

....

41 Sūra 6. Al-An'am, verse 78.

Understand that these are but stages that you are meant to surpass! In the *khulwa*, we condensed all this for you, gathered it into a ring, which we then threw, and asked you to illuminate it with the light of the Lord. You did so, and informed us that the room had transformed for you into light upon light, with the illumination engulfing everything. That's when we told you: "Well done, now leave, your *khulwa* here is complete."

But alas, you refused to grasp the deeper message. After exiting the *khulwa*, you spent years in our presence, causing a tumult of unnecessary confusion. All for what? What kind of intellect hides in this *nāṣiya*? Will you finally end up understanding something?

Instead of telling us that you "merely" perceived a blue light, understand that the truth (*ḥaqīqa*) is incredibly simple and direct: this is the light of *al-muḥīt* (The All-Encompassing). If you contemplate this, you will immediately recall the verse, **"And He encompasses everything."**[42] So, instead of whining about seeing a "blue" light rather than forms and images, voice your gratitude with an *al-Ḥamdulilah*. Realize that being in the presence of The All-Encompassing is infinitely more profound than any barrier you conjure between you and Him.

We bid you farewell.

....

42 Sūra 57. Al-Hadid, verses 5-6. And Sūra 6. Al-An'am, verse 59.

31.
In the First Point of Sayyiduna Adam,
Three Types of Trials Will Fall upon You

The *nāṣiya* (the spiritual forelock) will consistently present you with images, sometimes of stones, sometimes of men. Yet some of you declare, "I don't want them. I only desire the *alif al-aḥmadī*. I must follow this *alif al-aḥmadī* step by step..."

But initially, what will the Shaykh tell me?

On which source (*manba'*) of the *alif* should I focus?

The *wilāya* (sainthood), the Shaykh informs me, is the isthmus (*barzakh*, the realm between the physical and the spiritual). It represents balance and perfect harmony. If I achieve this state of balance and flawless harmony of *wilāya*, then I have nothing more to pursue: I am a *Walī*!

So, on what should I concentrate?

I will work on the *naba'* (news) of the *nubuwwa* (prophecy).

But concretely, what does the *nubuwwa* represent for me?

It is that which I receive from the *naba'* of the Prophets (*anbiyā'*), within the *malakūt* (the angelic realm), based on their stories (*qaṣaṣ*). In this phase, I am working on the Prophets. I am immersing myself in the spiritual presence (*ḥadhra*) of the *naba' al-`adhīm* (the great news).

Now, who is the first Prophet?

It's Adam ﷺ!

What is special about Sayyiduna Adam ﷺ?

"He was 70 meters tall..."

So what? How is this information useful to you?

Will he come and plow the field alongside you?

When you recount the story of Sayyiduna Adam ﷺ, mentioning that he was 70 meters tall and that he covered 100 meter in a single stride, to what end? Is he akin to a 4x4 that you'll utilize for travel? What exactly are you envisioning from Adam ﷺ with this perspective?

No, Adam ﷺ should be perceived as the embodiment of *asmā' Allah al-ḥusna* (the beautiful names of Allah ﷻ). He is the source of the divine names. He is the point that we refer to as "*`ilm al-asmā*'" - the knowledge of divine names. And this foundational point, the knowledge of names, is what I must possess.

And what is the first step of the science of divine names?

It's the niche (*mishkāt*): I must therefore be the holder of the *mishkāt* of `ilm al-asmā'. That is, I must be certain that the *hawiyya* (the sphere—*hā'*—of divine identity) unites all of the science of divine names. Here is the first exemplification (*mathal*).

But, if I perceive the *hawiyya* as the synthesis of the science of divine names, if I regard it as the grandest conceivable union of all names, then upon witnessing it, would I dare say: "I don't see the light"?

Go ahead and speak now, Sidi Hassan. Yes! You who say, "I do not see the light..." You see the entirety of all the names. Allah ﷻ has made you a ring, which He has placed on your heart like a seal! If you do not want this seal, we can erase it and stamp something else in its place. But know that there are only two possible stamps: truthful (*ṣiddīq*) or liar (*kādhib*). Choose which one you want; that's it.

Therefore, if the Lord has stamped your heart with the *mishkāt* of the names, know that you are following the prophecy of Adam ﷺ. At that moment, you should study your *nafs* (ego). This means that you are either *barzakhī* (intermediary) like Sayyiduna Shīth ﷺ, or you are molded in the image of the one who sacrificed himself out of love for Allah ﷻ, longing to return to Him—that is, in the likeness of Sayyiduna Habīl (Abel). Alternatively, if you heed your *nāṣiya*, you become Qabīl (Cain).

These three points are what you encounter in the very first point of Sayyiduna Adam ﷺ. This sets the stage for the type of trial that will befall you. But... what is exactly this trial we refer to?

Clearly:

– Either I work, I sell my *nafs* (ego) and my possessions for my spirit. In this case, I am Habīl. I become indifferent to everything else. The only aspect that holds significance to me is this *mishkāt* of the prophecy, of which I too am a point.

– Or I observe the other disciples with envy. "Oh, so-and-so has two secrets... so-and-so has three..." "Oh, this one accompanies the Shaykh while I remain here..." This mindset reflects Qabīl. It's the awakening of Qabīl within.

– Or, I am present, I work, and in this endeavor, the Lord will groom me, just like Adam ﷵ, for the knowledge of the divine names, leading me to acquire a portion of this knowledge.

Now, present your heart for evaluation in the light of this *mishkāt*! Position your heart on this three-tiered scale and reveal to us your identity: Are you Qabīl, Habīl, or Shīth?

Who is Shīth ﷵ?

He is the one who took a verse (*āya*), a name (*ism*), an interpretation (*tafsīr*), or an explanation from the Shaykh, then he started reflecting and working on it, setting all else aside. His entire love is reserved for this verse, staying up nights pondering its implications. Continuously he wonders, "Why did the Shaykh say this... there must be a profound secret here..." This individual is recognized as Shīth.

And Habīl, who is he?

Habīl ﷵ represents the one who is immersed in worship (*`ibāda*) and in giving of his wealth (*nafaqa*).

And Qabīl?

Qabīl is preoccupied observing those considered "mad." Referring to the hadith: "Praise Allah ﷻ until they declare: 'He has lost his mind!'" His attention is fixated on them, questioning their practices of *dhikr* (remembrance). If you try, for instance, rousing your brother at dawn, he would retort: "Let him rest, he's fine. Pursue your own *dhikr* and refrain from meddling." Essentially, he mimics the actions of *Iblīs* (Satan). "Don't disturb him, he's unwell, he has a fever... he was up all night watching a movie, he's drained...

wait until the *ādhān* (call to prayer) to wake him." This is the hallmark of Qabīl!

Thus, determine your position among these three.

32.
Understanding
Your Awakened Visions (*mushāhadāt*): How?

When a message (*risāla*) arrives, it is, in reality, inconceivable that we wouldn't understand its meaning. The idea that the Lord would send a message to someone incapable of grasping it is unthinkable. Whenever the Lord dispatches a sign, a hint, or something to a seeker, He never conveys anything beyond their capacity to understand. However, some things you might understand in the present moment, while others might take longer. You may need a week or even a month before you fully comprehend the message.

So, how can we be certain we understand the message as soon as it arrives? How do we interpret what we witness immediately, without delay?

Immediate understanding necessitates being among those who have devotedly adhered to their *wird*, their *adhkār*, and all their daily religious obligations. In contrast, an individual who neglects and forsakes his duties will experience a delay in comprehending the messages sent to him. Thus, it's not merely about seeing for the sake of seeing, but rather understanding what we witness.

Take, for instance, the scenario where your father sends you to the market. You might need a comprehensive list: two pounds of potatoes, one pound of this, three of that... However, if you routinely go to the market, you'll eventually discern what you must buy without constantly consulting your list. The underlying assumption is that after working for your father for an extended period, you've come to learn and understand his expectations without the need for explicit verbal or written instructions. All he might need to do is give you a certain look, and you immediately grasp his intentions. Alternatively, he hands you a specific amount of money, and you intuitively discern what he expects you to purchase.

The same principle applies: the more experience you gather in nurturing your relationship with the Lord, the deeper your understanding becomes of what this bond demands from you, in relation to Him. As for the Lord, He undoubtedly knows perfectly what resides within us; He is All-Knowing. However, we too must know. We need to understand, not what is in Him, but what lies within ourselves.

Thus, the truths of our inner selves will be unveiled to us, proportionally, based on how we maintain our relationship with our Lord. If He chooses to reveal this *ḥaqīqa* to us and we accept it as it is—meaning, if it aligns with what the Creator expects from His creatures—then we listen and obey. But if it contradicts divine laws, it becomes our responsibility to recognize that the issue lies within us. We then must take necessary actions to change and rectify ourselves, as this inherent problem is what may lead us to neglect and renounce obedience to the Lord and adherence to the teachings brought by al-Mustafa ﷺ.

33.
As Long as You Are Witnessing Worldly Things, You Aren't Witnessing Your Lord!

Allah says in the holy Quran: **"[Some] faces, that Day, will be radiant, looking at their Lord."**[43]

And you, of course, wish to be one of those faces that will gaze upon their Lord, don't you?

The challenge is that as long as you remain preoccupied with the images and apparent forms of this world, you aren't prepared to behold the Face of your Lord. You, you gaze upon stones and idols; and you perceive mere planets in the heavens. Do you grasp the gravity of this?

In this regard, you are essentially a face beholding emptiness. Yet, you yearn to be a face that witnesses that which is everlasting (*al-baqā'*). To become such a face, one that perceives *al-baqā'*, you must transform into light yourself. You need to shed your appearance, your form, your very image. Should you retain even a single atom of these, you will be denied the sight of the Face of Allah ﷻ.

When the Messenger of Allah ﷺ was posed with the question, "Will we see our Lord on the Last Day?" He

....

43   Sūra 75. Al-Qayamah, verses 22-23.

responded, "Do you find difficulty in seeing the sun when no clouds obscure it?" To which the companions responded, "No, O Messenger of Allah ﷺ!"

Therefore, gaze upon the sky at noon on a cloudless day. Observe it intently... Do any images manifest before you? The answer is no; only sunlight graces your sight. You won't distinguish your spouse, your children, or anything else. And, if you persistently stare at it and subsequently cast your eyes downward to the earth, you will perceive nothing. Your vision will be dominated by a luminous reflection that engulfs all in its path. This is the essence of the question, "Do you find it hard to see the sun when no cloud obscures it?"

Continuing the hadith, the Messenger of Allah ﷺ further inquired: "Do you find difficulty in seeing the moon on a clear full moon night?" This isn't a reference to the crescent moon but to the full moon—specifically the moon on the nights of the 13th, 14th, and 15th of the lunar month. On such nights, when the moon is at its fullest and most luminous, and you find yourself in a desolate locale, can you discern anything other than the moon?

No, all that captivates your sight is the moon and the light it radiates.

In this world, you should only see the sun and the moon. Not the trees, not the seas, not the valleys... only the sun and the moon. Do you not claim to follow the Sunna? Or will you argue that this isn't the Sunna, that the hadith is weak (*da`if*), and that it's an innovation (*bid`a*)? So, what isn't an innovation? What else will you look at? Perhaps just the *ka'ba*? The *ka'ba* that an individual named Dhū al-Suwayqayn will eventually destroy. And when it's completely demolished, what will you worship then?

Therefore, seek the truth here, now, immediately!

Right here, you should have a sun or a moon that never sets, that never leaves you, from morning to night, and from night to morning. And don't be hypocritical with me by saying, "but in your Tariqa, do you worship the moon or what?" No, there is no greater worshipper of the moon than you. Because you are the one attached to apparent forms, not us. We desire the moon that never disappears. We want the sun that never fades, and that turns your night into day! As the Messenger of Allah ﷺ said, "I have left you on the bright path: its night is no different from its day, and only he who is destined for doom deviates from it."

But not you. You always seem to have a problem. That's why, when you begin to experience divine manifestations (*tajalliyāt*) and glimpse a mere crescent moon, you imagine yourself to be among the spiritually elevated. But that's not true. You should work until you achieve the vision of a full moon. To reach the full moon (*badr*) from the crescent (*hilāl*), you need 14 days (stages).

And what do these 14 days (stages) represent?

They represent the 14 letters of light (the *qawāsim* of the Quran), that you need to have united in your heart! Therefore, you must become a *qasam* among the *qawāsim* of the Quran. Then, and only then, you will have a *badr* moon.

And to have a sun, you must be a Quran. Meaning you must have completed the other 15 days to complete the lunar month and the full lunar cycle. Only then will the sun appear to you. And then, indeed, you will become a face that beholds eternity (*al-baqā'*).

How will you then perceive the world and those in it?

The world and its inhabitants will become akin to the hypocrite in your eyes. For you will cast them behind you. The entirety of the world and all that it encompasses, you will throw it behind you. You will be among those whose **"light will run before them and on their right hands. Good news for you: gardens of Paradise..."**[44]

But what are these gardens of Paradise?

They are the living sciences, descending upon you like rain in the very moment, a flow from the Creator Himself.

Then, your heart and your speech will align closest to the original pact with the Lord. There are no images here. The images are behind you; they are the ones who plead, **"Wait, let us borrow some of your light!"** You will respond, **"Back off! Go away! Go back and seek the light."**[45] Depart, go far, very far... for all this distance that separates us is still not enough. Go away, for I have divorced you three times. I left you in this world for whoever will come after me.

44 Sūra 57. Al-Hadīd, verse 12.
45 Sūra 57. Al-Hadīd, verses 12-13.

34.
Gratitude for Allah's Blessings

Allah ﷻ says: **"And be grateful for the blessings of Allah, if it is Him that you worship."**[46] In this verse lies the command to thank Allah ﷻ. But how to truly thank Him?

Showing gratitude for the blessings He has bestowed upon us is not about repeating a phrase a certain number of times with the tongue, without reality (*ḥaqīqa*) in the heart. Rather, the way to show gratitude for Allah's ﷻ blessings is by giving utmost importance to His favors and sanctifying them. The more importance we place on Allah's ﷻ blessings within us, the more we will realize the state of gratitude. The Prophet ﷺ prayed every night to the point that his feet cracked. When asked why he subjected himself to such hardship, he answered, "Should I not be a grateful servant?"

Gratitude originates from the heart, not merely from the tongue. It is entirely possible for a servant to spend his nights repeating *"al-ḥamdu lillahi wa shukru lillah"* without truly acknowledging his Lord's favors. From this understanding comes the directive not to squander the blessings which Allah ﷻ has generously granted us:

....

46 Sūra 16. An-Nahl, verse 114.

"And do not waste unjustly: the wasteful are akin to the devils, and the Devil is ever ungrateful to his Lord."[47]

O disciple, if your vision of the divine Light (the most supreme of all blessings that can be granted to a man) is realized without you attributing significance to it, then know that you have no stake in the state of gratitude towards your Lord. Even if you express your gratitude with your tongue, in prostration, at least 200 times a day, it holds little weight. Hence, do not anticipate any growth within yourself, nor any ascension to the essence of the Spirit: **"Your Lord proclaimed: 'If you are grateful, I will surely enhance [My blessings] for you. But if you deny [My blessings], indeed, My punishment is severe.'"**[48]

And know, O disciple, that no matter what transpires, you will never be able to express gratitude as it truly should be. The Prophet ﷺ alluded to this inherent incapacity (`ajz) within God's creation towards the Creator, saying: "I cannot praise You as You deserve; You are as You have praised Yourself." And Allah ﷻ declares: **"They do not value Allah ﷻ as He deserves (*Haqqa qadrihi*)."**[49] This implies that, despite all the reverence (*ta`dhīm*) we can offer for what emanates from Allah ﷻ, we remain unable to esteem Him as He truly deserves (*taqdīr*).

Now, know, disciple, that the selves that dread death the most are the ones that despise the Shaykh the most.

....

47   Sūra 17. Al-Isra, verse 27.
48   Sūra 14. Ibrahim, verse 7.
49   Sūra 6. Al-An'am, verse 91.

The latter continually challenges individuals' egos, guiding them towards the knowledge and realization of their true essence. Nothing in the world brings a disciple closer to Allah ﷻ, therefore to being grateful to Him, than moments spent in the presence of a `ārif billah`: this is arguably the pinnacle of worship. If you lack this opportunity, the sole act that can match the merit of these sessions is to retreat and engage in continuous *dhikr*, day and night, without pause. Yet, it's evident that such unwavering dedication is obviously beyond your reach...

The Prophet ﷺ proclaimed: "Deeds are only as valuable as their intentions." So, introspect: Why do you seek the company of a Shaykh? What do you genuinely hope to gain from this companionship? Is it the profound Knowledge of Allah ﷻ... or merely matters tied to this lower world?

Upon reflecting on these questions, understand that the key to progress on the Sufi Path is to consistently hold your Shaykh in high regard. The moment a negative sentiment takes root in your heart towards him, even if he never harbored one against you, recognize that there may be no true virtue within you.

Furthermore, comprehend that a Shaykh is not elevated amongst people solely to guide each one towards *ma`rifa*, the Knowledge of Allah ﷻ. This is a common misconception. The primary, singular purpose of the Shaykh is to help you know yourself.

If you are a believer and a beloved of Allah ﷻ, the Shaykh will allow you to remove the veils that prevent you from realizing this knowledge. And if you are a hypocrite, the Shaykh will make you aware of it. And if you flee and decide to leave the Path of Allah ﷺ, know that it is not the Shaykh you are fleeing, but rather your own image that is reflected in him. In the hadith: "The believer *(al-mūmin)* is the mirror of his brother." Here we are talking about *al-mūmin*, which translates as the believer, and which especially refers to the man who has fully realized himself in the divine Name *Al-Mūmin*. This represents a profoundly elevated spiritual state. Hence, refrain from presuming that every Muslim can serve as that authentic mirror revealing and allowing you to know your true self.

The `ārif billah* is a Sun, yet people do not see it because this Sun is obscured by clouds. If the clouds were to dissipate and this Sun revealed to everyone's eyes, all would recognize it. Yet, this is the nature of things: when Allah ﷺ desires good for one of His servants, He lifts some of these veils, allowing him to perceive the reality of the `ārif.* On the other hand, when He wishes to distance a servant, He increases their veils, leaving them in a state of blindness and heedlessness. This dynamic reveals the divine wisdom behind the unveiling of spiritual states *(ahwāl)*. The divine intent isn't to expose the `ārif billah* to the world. For you, as a seeker, your mission is to genuinely strive towards self-awareness. Through this process of self-discovery and recognition, you inch closer to understanding the reality of Allah ﷺ and His creation.

The `ārif billah* serves as a Sun that can illuminate your path. However, its light only touches you if you're prepared to see past the clouds of your preconceptions and ego-driven desires. This journey into spirituality demands humility, sincerity, and an unwavering commitment to cleanse your heart. Your paramount objective in this path shouldn't anchor to the material realm but to the pursuit of knowledge of Allah ﷻ. If you harbor intentions other than this, it would be wise to reconsider and introspect your true purpose on this spiritual path. Remember, actions are judged by their intentions, as taught by the Prophet ﷺ.

35.
Knowing Allah through
His Sublime Beauty

Let's discuss "*al-jamāl*," or the divine beauty of the Creator. I want to emphasize that it is impossible to praise Allah ﷻ without understanding His beauty. Only when one's self-awareness is extinguished, when the light of faith dispels the constructs of time and space, and when the disciple perceives neither past nor future, neither up nor down, can the depth of the verse **"Whichever way you turn, there is the Face of Allah ﷻ"**[50] be fully grasped. To witness and savor this reality, Allah ﷻ has provided us a singular and unparalleled path: adhering to the supreme example, the Sunna of our Prophet ﷺ.

Aisha, the mother of the believers ﵂, narrates:

> The beginning of the Divine revelation to Allah's Messenger ﷺ was in the form of righteous dreams which came true like bright daylight, and then the love of seclusion was bestowed upon him. He used to go in seclusion in the cave of Ḥira where he used to worship Allah ﷻ continuously for many days before his desire to see his family. He used to take

....

50   Sūra 2. Al-Baqarah, verse 115.

with him the journey food for the stay and then come back to (his wife) Khadīja to take his food likewise again till suddenly the Truth descended upon him while he was in the cave of Ḥira.

The inaugural Sunna, thus established, involved seclusion in a cave, being alone with oneself to gain an understanding of one's Creator, in line with the axiom: "He who knows himself, knows his Lord." The *khulwa*, or spiritual retreat, represents the exclusive and ultimate gateway to the Supreme Knowledge of the Lord of the worlds. It also functions as a one-way portal, a door that, once traversed, precludes any return. When the disciple acknowledges his non-existence and recognizes the existence of the One, without beginning or end, he cannot revert to relying on what is merely illusory. Whoever crosses this threshold will discover Allah ﷻ: how then can one who has known Allah ﷻ return to His creation?

The Prophets attained the `aïn al-wujūd* (essential source of existence), in line with their respective stations, during their *khulwa*. `Aïn al-wujūd* presented itself to Sayyiduna Dawūd ﷵ as a six-pointed luminous star, to Sayyiduna Mūsa ﷵ as a five-pointed star, and Sayyiduna Muhammad ﷺ received the *Basmala* in its *marqūm* form (i.e., three points forming a triangle). The Messenger of Allah ﷺ said in a hadith: "Contemplate Allah's creation, but not His Essence." We all sail the same sea, yet each perceives his proximity to his Lord based on his inner self... Indeed, the people of Allah ﷻ cannot directly express His Grandeur. They instead turn to creation, using it as a conduit to express their love for the Creator. Some have depicted the rising dawn, others have recounted a woman's love, while others have compared the illumination of their hearts to the sight of the sun or moon... and so on. When divine light fills the hearts of the Devotees and they recognize they're treading on this Light, they remove their shoes, emulating the example of Sayyiduna Mūsa ﷺ: **"When he arrived at the location, he heard: 'Mūsa! I am your Lord. Remove your sandals; you are in the sacred valley Tuwā.'"**[51] In a similar vein, it's recounted that Imam Malik ﷺ walked barefoot in Medina, maintaining he could not step his sandals on the ground trodden by the Messenger of Allah ﷺ. Those who assume this practice was limited to the blessed city of the Prophet ﷺ are mistaken: Imam Malik ﷺ walked barefoot wherever he traveled, as the Light of the beloved is boundless, except in a heart obscured by the physical forms.

Know, disciple, that by worshipping Allah ﷺ through *al-jamāl*, one savors the essence of prayer and fasting. The love of *al-jamāl* can only blossom in hearts through *nūr al-jamāl*. This Light serves as a mirror. The Messenger of Allah ﷺ, who is referred to as a Light in the Quran, tells us: "The believer is the mirror of the believer, and the believer is the brother of the believer." The quintessential believer is the Prophet ﷺ himself, whom the Companions witnessed weeping days before his passing. When they asked, "What makes you cry, O Messenger of Allah ﷺ?" He responded: "I miss my broth-

....

51 Sūra 20. Taha, verse 12.

ers!" Let us deeply understand who the beloved's brothers ﷺ are...

The disciple who knows Allah ﷻ through *al-jamāl* will relish the true sweetness of *dhikr*. As night descends, he will turn to his Lord, using the sky as a blanket, and begin to converse with the stars one by one... and he will learn how each of them speaks of the Creator. The Devotee enveloped in divine Light will perceive only *al-jamāl* in everything. Taking off his sandals, he will tread upon thorns and stones without sensing any pain, his senses overwhelmed by the manifestations of his Lord's sublime beauty.

I caution you: those who love Allah ﷻ should prepare to be tested... those who love the Messenger of Allah ﷺ should be ready to embrace poverty... and those who love Sayyiduna Ali ؓ should brace for adversaries to confront them. As for the one who professes love for Allah ﷻ but is not severely tested in life, the one who claims love for His Messenger yet doesn't endure poverty, or the one who avows love for Sayyiduna Ali ؓ without having adversaries challenge his path to truth, know that this person is simply being untruthful.

36.
"Ask the People of Remembrance (*dhikr*),
if You Do not Know"

Allah ﷻ says, "**And We sent not before you, [O Muhammad], except men to whom We revealed, so ask the people of remembrance (*dhikr*) if you do not know.**"[52]

By mentioning *dhikr*, Allah ﷻ signifies the gateway to the Divine Presence and the heralding of Divine Witnessing, the Secret of theophanies, the portal of spiritual revelations, the water of ablutions that cleanses both from the minor impurities of worldly contingencies and the major impurity of sensory perceptions. It is through *dhikr* that individuals find success in this world and honor in the hereafter. Encouraging us to engage in *dhikr* and lauding those who practice it, the Prophet ﷺ said: "The *Mufarridūn* have outstripped (others)." When the Companions asked, "Who are the *Mufarridūn*, O Messenger of Allah?" He replied: "Those men and women who remember Allah abundantly (*adhākirīna Allaha kathīran wa dh'dhākirāt*)."

According to Abdullah ibn Baṣr ﷺ, a man approached saying, "O Messenger of Allah, the Laws of Islam are

....

52 Sūra 16. Al-Nahl, verse 43.

extensive; please guide me to something concise that I can adhere to." The Prophet ﷺ replied: "Ensure your tongue is always moistened with the *dhikr* of Allah ﷻ."

Abu Mūsa ﵁ reported that the Prophet ﷺ remarked, "The comparison between one who remembers his Lord and one who doesn't is akin to the living and the dead."

As narrated by Abu ad-Dardā' ﵁, the Prophet ﷺ inquired, "Would you like to learn of your most virtuous deeds? The deeds most pleasing to your Lord, elevating your ranks, which are more valuable than gifting gold, worldly goods, or even facing your foe in combat where you strike him, and he strikes you?" The Companions asked, "What is it, O Messenger of Allah?" He responded, "The *dhikr* of Allah ﷻ."

Understand, disciple, that the people of *dhikr* stand foremost in the encompassing Glory of the Divine. They are a mercy for the people on earth. Those who join their gatherings are shielded from harm, and those who ally with them remain unoppressed. The lowest in social rank among them are esteemed in the eyes of Allah ﷻ, and those looked down upon by society are revered by Him. Their state of Divine Presence (*ḥāl*) illuminates and purifies their hearts, setting aside all but Him, readying themselves to embrace the Magnificence of the Master of all. Their *dhikr* establishes a luminous bond unbroken by the perils of heedlessness and forgetfulness. Neither trade nor commerce diverts them from the *dhikr* of Allah ﷻ, who guides, **"Stay patient with those who invoke their Lord at dawn and dusk, seeking His Countenance. Do not let your gaze shift from them, desiring worldly allurements. Do not follow the one** whose heart is oblivious to Our remembrance, who follows whims, and whose affairs are in disarray."[53]

Furthermore, Allah ﷻ emphasized the eminence of the people of *dhikr* in the degrees of Proximity, stating: "The Muslim men and women, the believing men and women, the obedient, the truthful, the patient, the humble, the charitable, the fasting, the chaste men and women, and those men and women who remember Allah often - for them Allah has prepared forgiveness and a magnificent reward."[54]

This verse enumerates ten degrees, with *dhikr* being the noblest and highest among them. Consider, therefore, may you be guided, how the Real (*Al-Ḥaqq*) has commanded us to ask the people of *dhikr*, as He has chosen and elected them among all the people of knowledge. For it is the people of *dhikr* who are truly the people of knowledge (*`ilm*): they are those who act according to what they have been taught by the Lord and His Messenger ﷺ, the ones who understand the twists and turns of the *nafs*, the witnesses of the divine Power (*qudra*) beyond the veil of Wisdom, and those who plunge into the Oceans of Lordly Knowledge.

If you have a question, turn to the people of Light, for they are the custodians of the remedy leading to the Presence of the Real. Their proximity is a mercy, and entrance into their presence is both a favor and a divine blessing.

....

53 Sūra 18. Al-Kahf, verse 28.
54 Sūra 33. Al-Ahzab, verse 35.

Ask those whose being is perpetually imbued with the state of Presence (*ḥuḍūr*), those whose Knowledge by Allah ﷻ (*ma`rifa billah*) is established, those who have read, by the Name of their Lord, the reality of their own souls. For when they know it, they know by it the entirety of all souls. Thus, no inner ailment can remain concealed from them. Their antidotes are the Lights of Proximity, offering healing from the darkness of multiplicity and the created world.

And may Allah ﷻ reward our Shaykh Sidi al-Būzīdī (*Quddisa Sirruh*) who said in verse:

Every jurist is knowledgeable
about the obligations (farḍ) and Sunna

Yet my Knowledge is boundless,
endless

I am the one who provides drink,
and the wine is mine

I am the one who unveils,
and the Presence is mine

How many ignorant have come
and entered my Path

They have become people of profound meanings,
kings of divine providence

Remove your sandals and erase your selfhood,
if you wish to meet me

If you wish to know us:
I am the Source (`aïn) of Life

I am the realization itself (`aïn at-taḥqīq),
oh you who ask to see me

I am the course of the Path,
and the universe is in my Grasp (qabḍatī)

The universe is like a mirage,
as the verse describes

like dust dispersed in the wind,
among the people of Realities

From the Oceans of the Realm of Invincibility (jabarūt),
my Point has emerged

It was colored by the physical contingencies (nāsūt),
and the Secret of the Realm of Divine Sovereignty
(malakūt)

37.
Knowledge

Mawlana ibn `Āshir al-Mālikī said in his famous poem:

*And the first obligation incumbent upon every
responsible person (mukallaf),*

Is to know the Real and the Messengers

The first obligation of the individual who has reached the age of reason is to know Allah ﷻ and His Messenger ﷺ, or in other words: the Knowledge of the dual testimony (*shahāda*), a deep and true Knowledge. The gateway to the religion of Allah ﷻ is thus this dual testimony. And the gateway out of this lower world to the religion of Allah ﷻ is this dual testimony.

Knowledge is the reality of what forms the foundation of reverential fear, which is the theophanic mount and the object of contemplation for Sufi Scholars. Allah ﷻ says, "**Among His servants, only the Scholars fear Allah. Indeed, Allah is Most Powerful and Most Forgiving.**"[55] So consider, may Allah ﷻ have mercy on you, how the Real has associated Knowledge with divine fear

....

55 Sūra 35. Al-Fātir, verse 28.

(*khashya*), to show us the link between these two spiritual stations. Therefore, the one whose knowledge of Allah ﷻ increases, his fear of Him will also increase. In this sense, we find an authentic word reported from the master of creation ﷺ: "By Allah ﷻ, I am among them the most knowledgeable of Allah ﷻ, and the one who fears Him the most."

The first sign of reverential fear manifesting in the servant is, on one hand, the act of considering others with a vision that magnifies them, contemplating the divine spiritual flow circulating within them... and on the other hand, the act of diminishing and debasing one's ego, always striving to conform to the divine Law and remaining constantly in a state nourished by fear. This is the state of perfectly realized knowers (*`ārifīn*), as it is the celestial mount (*burāq*) towards divine Knowledge, subtly oscillating between the degree of imaginative representation and that of gnostic theophany.

In al-Baḥr al-Madīd, Imam ibn `Ajība reports:

> Al-Rabī` ibn Anas said: "the one who does not fear Allah ﷻ is not a Scholar." As for ibn 'Abbas, he said in the exegesis of this verse: "Asceticism is sufficient as knowledge." And ibn Mas`ūd said: "the fear of Allah ﷻ is enough as knowledge, and excuses are enough as ignorance." And in the Hikam: "The best of sciences is the one that is accompanied by fear." And in at-Tanwīr: "Know that, wherever it is mentioned in the Book or in the Sunna, knowledge (*`ilm*) refers to beneficial knowledge, the one that is accompanied by fear, surrounded by concern."

Allah ﷻ says, **"Among His servants, only the Scholars fear Allah ﷻ."** Here He ﷻ indicates that fear is necessarily accompanied by Knowledge, and from this we understand that the Scholars are in reality the people of reverential fear.

Shaykh ibn `Abbad al-Rundi ﷺ said:

> And know that the beneficial Knowledge, about which there is unanimity both among the early generations and those who followed them, is the Knowledge that leads its holder to fear and dread, the Knowledge that takes him to humility and self-debasement, to conformity to the characteristics of faith, as well as, on the other hand, to the rejection of this lower world and to asceticism, making him prefer the hereafter, and all this in conformity with the respect required towards Allah ﷻ, as well as all the other noble characteristics of the Sunna.

And in Lata̓if al-Minan, it is stated:

> The sign of the Knowledge demanded by Allah ﷻ is fear. And the sign of fear is the servant's conformity to what is commanded of him. As for knowledge that is accompanied by a desire for this lower world, deference towards the people who possess the greatest part of it, and a desire to apply oneself to imitate them, to accumulate, hoard, without ever worrying about the consequences, forgetting the hereafter... there is no knowledge more remote than

this from what is described as the inheritance of the Prophets!

Could the inheritance go to the heir without him fully conforming to the description of the one from whom he inherits? An example of one of the Scholars, whose description is this, is like a candle: it enlightens others, but burns itself. Allah ﷻ made the knowledge taught to such a person a proof (*ḥujja*) against him and a cause for increasing his punishment.

In the verse **"Only the Scholars fear Allah ﷻ among His servants,"** in its Arabic version, the mention of the Name of Allah ﷻ precedes that of the Scholars, suggesting that only the Scholars truly fear Allah ﷻ. If the verse had been phrased differently (by preceding the mention of Scholars with the Divine Name), the meaning would have been that the Scholars fear only Allah ﷻ.

In a Prophetic hadith: "On the Day of Judgement, Allah ﷻ will address the Scholars, when He takes His place (literally: sits) on His pedestal (*Kursī*) to pass judgement on His servants: 'I certainly placed in you My Knowledge and My Discernment because I want to forgive you for what is in you, and I care little about it.'"

Al-Mundhirī commented: "consider therefore the Divine Word: 'My Knowledge and My Discernment.' It is clear and evident that this is not about the common knowledge of the majority of people of this era devoid of Knowledge by Him and sincerity (*ikhlās*)."

In another version of this hadith: "I certainly placed in you My Wisdom for a good that I want for you: enter Paradise, despite what is in you."

And he ﷺ also said: "On the Day of Judgement, the ink of the Scholars will be weighed, as well as the blood of the martyrs, but it is the ink of the Scholars that will prevail over the blood of the martyrs."

Esoteric indication:

The Scholars are to be considered in two distinct groups. On the one hand, the Scholars of Allah's ﷻ Laws, and on the other hand, the Scholars by Allah ﷻ. The Scholars of Allah's ﷻ Laws fear His anger and His punishment, while the Scholars by Allah ﷻ fear His distance and being veiled from Him. The Scholars of Allah's ﷻ Laws fear to commit sins, while the Scholars by Allah ﷻ fear to lack decorum in the Presence of the Supreme Sovereign. The fear of the Scholars by Allah ﷻ is thus denser and stronger. They take their Knowledge from Allah ﷻ, unlike the Scholars of Law who take their Knowledge from the dead.

Shaykh Abu Yazīd al-Bustāmī (*Quddisa Sirruh*) remarked on the scholars who rely on chains of transmission (*riwāyah*): "These are poor people whose Knowledge is taken from dead person to another dead person. As for us, we draw our Knowledge from the Ever-Living who never dies."

Now, regarding the difference between the terms *khawf, rahba* and *khashya: Khawf* denotes the fear of punishment, *rahba* the fear of blame, and *khashya* the fear of distance.

Al-Qushayri says: "The difference between the terms *rahba* and *khashya* is that the first refers to a fear that forces the one affected by it to flee and panic. As for *khashya*, on the contrary, it has the effect of slowing down the one who is affected by it, and thus he remains with Allah ﷻ. *Khashya* therefore prevails over *rahba*."

The term *khawf* belongs to faith (*īmān*). Indeed, Allah ﷻ says: **"And fear Me (*khawf*) if you are believers."**[56] The term *khashya* belongs to Knowledge and Divine Grandeur.

The exoteric scholar fears (*khawf*) of failing to fulfill the rights his Lord holds over him. In contrast, the knower fears (*khashya*) breaching the proper decorum and respect he owes to Him; he is wary of erring at an inappropriate moment, uttering a misplaced word, or neglecting the priority good deeds.

Al-Wartajabī ﷺ said:

> The term *khawf* (fear) is common among the people, while *khashya* (awe) is for the elite. And indeed, He has made *khashya* to be accompanied by Knowledge (`*ilm*), that is, the Knowledge through Allah ﷻ, linked to His Omnipotence, His Lordship, and the servitude devoted to Him. The reality of *khashya* is the descent of the nobility of the Truth into the hearts of the knowers (`*ārifīn*), combined with the glint of divine Magnificence and the vision of His Grandeur and Majesty. However, only one who delves into the witnessing of the pre-eternal and uncreated, the enduring and the eternal, can achieve this. As one's Knowledge through Allah ﷻ grows, so does his *khashya*, in

....

56   Sūra 3. Āl-`Imran, verse 175.

alignment with the Prophetic saying: "Among you, I am the most Knowledgeable through Allah ﷻ, and the one who feels awe (*khashya*) for Him the most." And in another hadith, it was asked: "O Messenger of Allah ﷺ, what is the best of deeds? He replied: Knowledge (*al-`ilm*). They asked: What Knowledge? He said: Knowledge through Allah ﷻ."

In the *Hikam* it is also said: "Beneficial Knowledge is that whose rays spread in the chest, and by which the veil of the heart is lifted."

Knowledge (`*ilm*) is therefore composed of the rays of gnosis (`*irfān*). As soon as its Lights spread in the heart, they dispel the veils of the the other (*al-ghayr*) and duality (*thunā'iyya*). The darkness of the created world fades away, and the Attributes of the Creator then appear. His Lights branch out in the heart, and this is what is referred to as beneficial Knowledge: the visualization of the Light of Allah ﷻ and His Messenger ﷺ.

The Real has indeed described Himself as Light, exalted be He:

Allah is the Light of the heavens and the earth. The exemplification of His light is like a niche within which is a lamp, The lamp is within glass, the glass as if it were a resplendent star, Lit from [the oil of] a blessed olive tree, Neither of the east nor of the west, Whose oil would almost glow even if untouched by fire. Light upon light. Allah guides to His light whom He wills.

And God presents examples for the people, and God is Knowing of all things.[57]

And He ﷻ described His Prophet ﷺ as a shining lamp: **"O Prophet! We have sent you as a witness, announcer, warner, calling to Allah, by His permission, and as a shining lamp."**[58]

The reality of Knowledge (`*ilm*) is nothing other than the embellishment by the Light of the Lordly Presence, manifesting itself in the form of the Lamp (*miṣbāḥ*) of Knowledge, in the Glass (*zujāja*) of our master the Messenger of Allah ﷺ. It is made apparent by the Niche (*mishkāt*) of inner and concealed revelation, through the Star (*kawkab*) of Union in the night preserving the Secret of all Secrets—a Light whose fuel comes from the Tree of the Secret, transcending all spatial dimensions.

And may Allah duly reward Imam al-Shafi`ī ﷺ, who said in a poem:

I complained to Wakī` about my bad memory
And he enjoined me to abandon sins

Informing me that Knowledge is Light
And the Light of Allah ﷻ is not gifted to the sinner

Knowledge (`*ilm*) is therefore Light, not a sequence of written lines. It is a Light by which one understands, exoterically and esoterically, what Allah ﷻ intends for everything.

....

57   Sūra 24. An-Nur, verse 35.
58   Sūra 33. Al-Ahzab, verses 45-46.

It is sanctified Water, descended from the heavens of the unseen (*ghayb*) upon the fertile lands that are the hearts of the believers.

The Prophet ﷺ thus said:

> The example of what Allah ﷻ has raised me with in terms of Guidance and Knowledge is like abundant rain that touches a land. A part of this land is good and apt to receive this water; on its surface, abundant pastures and herbs grow. Another part (of this land) is impermeable and retains water, so that Allah ﷻ benefits the people from it. They drink from it, water their herds, and cultivate their fields. This abundant rain also touches another part of the land: arid land that neither holds water nor grows any grass. This is the likeness, on one hand, of the one who learns the religion of Allah ﷻ, benefiting from what I have been raised with by studying and teaching it, and on the other hand, of the one who does not benefit from this and does not accept the Guidance of Allah ﷻ with which I was sent.

Consider, may Allah ﷻ have mercy on you, the way in which he, who does not speak under the effect of passion, has made the people of the Lights the true Scholars. They are the first group (from the first land), the holders of the reality of Knowledge. As for the second group, they only hold the form and "external appearance" of Knowledge. And finally, the third group is the group of those who have neither the reality of Knowledge, nor even its form.

The first group is made up of those who have welcomed the Water of Prophetic Knowledge into the fertile lands of their souls. Thus, what appeared from these lands became verdant under the influence of the profound meanings of Divine Names. Then, the fruits of Knowledge appeared on these lands. This land is the one that the Beloved ﷺ compared to the land that produced abundant pastures and herbs because its people welcomed the Water of Revelation from the world of the unseen (*ghayb*) into the fertile lands of their hearts. They grasped a true Knowledge of the descent of Names into Divine Attributes, the descent of Attributes into Acts, and the descent of Acts into Laws. They spoke to people according to their understanding and revealed, at every moment, what would be beneficial to the servants. And it was said of them:

> *Perform your ablutions with the Water of the ghayb,*
> *if you hold a Secret*
> *otherwise, perform dry ablution (tayammum)*
> *with earth or stone*

> *Take as imam the one of whom you are the imam*
> *and perform the fajr prayer at the beginning of `asr*

> *Such is the prayer of the Scholars by their Lord:*
> *if you are one of them,*
> *then sprinkle the firm land with the ocean*

The second group comprises those who have taken and absorbed the Water, and who have then dispensed it. This reflects the state of the people of the exoteric sciences, particularly in our present time. An individual memorizes, then reproduces what has been memorized, and nothing beyond that. The Beloved ﷺ characterized them, informing us that through them, the Real allowed others to benefit from their preservation of the Water of the *ghayb*. However, they derived no advantage for their own souls, apart from the reward accompanying this memorization. Thus, the reward is theirs, but the advantage of their memorization and their safeguarding of the Water of the *ghayb* is for the people of the first group; for they are the ones who can truly drink, irrigate, and cultivate.

Regarding the third group, it consists of those who are barren; those who neither hold onto the Water nor nurture pastures. In other terms, they have neither the reward of memorization nor the Secret preserving the inner Lights. May Allah ﷻ shield us from such a state.

Knowledge (`ilm*) is not merely about you memorizing and then flaunting your memorization, which would reduce you to a mere machine replaying a recording. Rather, Knowledge entails understanding the verse or the divine sign (*āya*), implementing it, and subsequently harvesting the yield of your efforts: a yield manifesting as Lights, through which you discern the Will of Allah ﷻ. Then, you can duly accord everyone their rightful due, embodying the finest etiquette, the superior spiritual states, and the most profound mystical experiences.

38.

The *Muraqqaʿa*, Symbol of the Universal Man
(*al-Insān al-Kāmil*)

Allah ﷻ says: "Do you not see that Allah sends rain from the sky, causing it to become springs [and rivers] on the earth? From this, He brings forth crops of diverse colors; after which they wither, and you observe them turning yellow, and then He reduces them to [scattered] debris. Truly, in this is a lesson for those with insight."[59]

O seeker desiring to meet and know your Lord, have you not observed that from a seemingly insignificant, colorless substance devoid of taste or smell, Allah ﷻ manifests the immense diversity of forms and colors that adorn creation? This is the analogy our Lord presents to describe the Universal Man, the *Walī*. He is the rare and unparalleled water of life that descends from spiritual realms to rejuvenate hearts, placing within them his boundless fruits. In this manner, he enables each confined perspective of the *nafs* to perceive the hue reflecting its profound *ḥaqīqa*. This understanding leads the disciple toward recognizing his Lord, echoing

....

59 Sūra 35. Al-Fatir, verse 27.

193

the prophetic saying: "He who knows his *nafs*, knows his Lord."

Yet, to partake in these fruits and this wisdom, the wayfarer (*sālik*) cannot be stagnant. He must perpetually aspire to draw nearer to his Lord, always in the *Walī's* presence, akin to planets orbiting the Sun. First and foremost, he needs to uphold his commitment: staying devoted to his *wird*, daily *sūras*, the regular recitation of his two *ḥizbs*[60] from the Quran, and the practice of *dhikr* during the final third of the night. Additionally, he should diligently follow each directive and every counsel from his Shaykh. If he remains steadfast, his journey will hasten, unveiling a profound Secret concealed within this command.

The discerning disciple will also emulate what the *Walī* cherishes, distancing himself from actions the *Walī* disapproves of. He will take to heart the praises the *Walī* bestows upon his disciples. In doing so, he progresses on his spiritual path by bringing together the different colors of the *muraqqa`a*, reflecting the various confined perspectives, until returning to the white of the absolute, thus becoming a perfect shadow of the Vicegerent of Allah.

In this regard, I say in one of my poems:

Tear the garment of the self through patching

You will dress in the garment of piety (at-taqwa) and vicegerency (al-khilāfati)

....

60 A *ḥizb* corresponds roughly to 10 pages in the modern *Madīna* codex (*muṣḥaf*).

This is the movement expected of the wayfarer. From this movement, the red of exclusive love for the Truth and the death of the *nafs* will ignite the disciple's heart. Like a glowing ember, he will return to the white. This is referenced in the continuation of the verse in which Allah ﷻ mentions mountains with white and red streaks, pointing to purity and divine love. They symbolize the persistent journey of the wayfarer aspiring to return to the source of creation, contrasted by totally black rocks due to their inertia in the divine pursuit.

Through this progression towards what the *Walī* approves, the colored *nafs* of the wayfarer will be purified until it becomes white, that is, colorless. This represents the harmonious assembly of the seven colors of the rainbow, termed the "mother colors" (*ummahāt al-alwān*). They allude to the realization of the seven degrees of readings of the Supreme Name reflecting the Divine Essence, Allah ﷻ.

The *muraqqa`a* is thus the attire of *al-Insān al-Kāmil.* It's the garment of the `*arifīn* (knowers), marking the junction between the *nafs* and the Spirit established by the *bay`a.* It's the robe of the *Wilāya* that unifies the heart and body of Man at the central point of the *Hā'* (ه) in the Name "Allah ﷻ". This union occurs as the wayfarer externally adorns the radiant reality illuminating his heart, heeding the prophetic directive. Indeed, the Prophet ﷺ stated, "Hold within yourself what you desire, for by Allah ﷻ neither a single soul nor a group can harbor an emotion internally without it manifesting outwardly. If it's virtuous, the manifestation will be virtuous; if wicked, the manifestation will be wicked."

From this understanding, we deduce that the manner in which one dresses is far from trivial. It's a vivid reflection of what one seeks to conceal within. This is a universal principle articulated by the Beloved ﷺ. Thus, an individual who lacks modesty, exposing their `awra publicly without a hint of shame, merely showcases a heart devoid of reverence, faith, and decorum in their Lord's presence. This aligns with the prophetic declaration: "Modesty is a facet of faith." On the flip side, an individual adorned in the *muraqqa`a* reflects a heart illuminated by the Muhammadan Light.

This Light represents the essential reality of the Universal Man (*al-Insān al-Kāmil*). Devoid of forms and colors, it signifies the starting point from which the diversity of creation sprang. It is like the Supreme Name, which, in the act of creation, brought forth the multifaceted, manifest and concealed, divine names. When this Light descends into the believer's inner self, it passes through the crystal (*zujāja*) of his heart. In that passage, it takes on the hues representing the divine names, by which the Lord unveils Himself to His servant's internal vision.

Now, disciple, let's discuss colors further. When you see blue, or the Light presents itself in blue, understand that it is the divine Name *Al-Muḥīt* (The All-encompassing) manifesting to you. We say this to the beginner in the Path but in reality the Name predominantly associated with the blue color is *Ar-Raḥmān* (The Most Gracious). To simplify the understanding of colors, we identified seven primary colors, termed *ummahāt* (mother colors). Hence, similarly, we tell the novice that the red color manifests the divine Name *Al-Mumīt* (The

Bringer of Death). But in truth, the Name that has the largest share in the red is *Al-Muḥib* (The All-Loving). Concerning yellow, we relate it to the Name *Adh-Dhāhir* (the Manifest). Yet, the dominant Name in yellow is *Al-Badī`* (The Incomparable Originator). Until the disciple has journeyed and reached understandings on the divine secrets, he won't be able to comprehend these subtleties.

Thus, we've categorized the colors into seven primary ones:

– Yellow: Symbolizes the divine name *Adh-Dhāhir*.

– Green: Represents the ninety-nine names of Allah ﷻ in synthesis (*ijmā`*).

– Blue: Reflects the divine name *Al-Muḥīt*.

– Red: Corresponds to the divine name *Al-Mumīt*.

– White: Is associated with the divine name *An-Nūr* (The Light).

– Purple: Represents the divine name *Al-Walī*.

– Black, when observed within the heart of the light, denotes the divine name *Al-Bātin* (The Concealed). We would never tie a divine name to darkness.

Teaching the novice about the science of colors and their meanings is an endless monumental task. This is not merely because today's disciples are woefully lacking in spiritual acumen, but also due to the sheer depth of this science. Indeed, each color contains seven sub-colors, and within those, myriad hues branch out endlessly. There are even colors, previously unseen by humanity, that were described in the Prophet's ﷺ hadith, where he observed unprecedented shades at *Sidrat al-Muntahā'*.

In light of this hadith, those who gaze upon the Light of the Real and perceive its multi-hued nature should externally don the colors constituting the *muraqqa`a.* As the heart's colors project onto the disciple's physique, their luminous realities will permeate his body, transforming him into a trace (*athar*) of the Prophet ﷺ. He becomes the manifest union of his niche (*mishkāt*) with its manifold reflections in the material realm (*mulk*). Thus, he will act as an immaculate perfect mirror through which each person can contemplate her own inner reality, manifested by one of the *muraqqa`a*'s colors.

39.
Guard your Heart!

If the seeker inclines towards anything other than Allah ﷻ, then the eye of their heart closes. This is how those who worshiped the calf and followed Sayyiduna Mūsa lost their inner vision, which had allowed them to distinguish between Truth and Falsehood. Similarly, when the eye of the heart closes in a seeker, it reflects in their behavior—you can observe them lacking respect and *adab* in the gatherings of remembrance, showing inadequate *ta`dhīm* for the *Ism al-Mufrad* (the Supreme Name of Allah) with which they undertook the spiritual seclusion (*khulwa*). Be cautious!

The Shaykh, just as he bestows, can also withhold. As he plants and sows, he likewise uproots. Mūlay al-`Arbī al-Darqāwī (*Quddisa Sirruh*) would become quite upset with anyone who stretched their legs during a gathering (instead of keeping them crossed). What, then, would he think of someone among you who permits himself to speak during a gathering of remembrance?

Feel ashamed before Allah ﷻ: a seeker might unknowingly become a hindrance for others on the Path, as ordinary people do not evaluate you by the number of Secrets you have unveiled or the intensity of Light within your heart, for these aspects are beyond their under-standing. Rather, they observe your behavior and every nuanced action, forming their judgments based on these.

Lastly, I've instructed you not to open your eyes during *dhikr*, ensuring that immediate surroundings don't divert your focus from the Ultimate Aim, aiding your swift transition from the material world to the domain of witnessed profound meanings. Therefore, don't open your eyes during *dhikr* until you attain a level where the vision of the heart merges with that of the eyes, making it inconsequential whether they remain shut or open.

40.
Is All Spirituality Equal? Beware of the Devil's Tricks!

O disciple, the spiritual paths we traverse are not all equivalent. They are neither equal nor identical, varying not just in their external manifestations but also at their cores. The experiences of those who practice them are not strictly comparable. These assertions, widely unpopular in our time, are nonetheless evident in both the sacred texts and the spiritual experiences of those who have excelled. Indeed, not all spiritualities are equal! Their shares of misguidance and truth are not identical, even though the concepts that emerge from them can be analogized.

Differences and Similarities:
Know Seeker of the Real that the spiritual lexicon varies from one tradition to another, from one religion to another, even from one order to another. A spiritual guide takes the liberty to use a term as he sees fit, giving it new life with unique explanations. Yet, it is highly likely that a contemporary master uses terms that have been employed by many masters of the past. The specifics of each Saintly Pole (*qutb*) accompany the he terms he uses, but the essence of what is indicated does not

change. Hence, what was designated as Truth (*ḥaqq*) at the dawn of Islam remains defined as Truth centuries later. If these masters were to converse in a meeting transcending the constraints of time and space, we would bear witness to their agreement on what the terms indicate. Each would be capable of bringing forth the uniqueness of what Allah ﷻ has revealed to them through these terms. This is how spirituality is experienced and transmitted within the Muslim community. Yet, if we expand our observations beyond the limits of our community and scrutinize the discourses of other spiritual figures, from Abrahamic or non-Abrahamic religions, we would see spiritual "concepts" that seem similar.

The domain of the human soul belongs to mankind, and it is normal for each religion, each tradition, to perceive it as they do. It is normal for truths and metaphysical realities to appear to people when they seek them. However, just because we may find a similar—or nearly similar—theoretical approach to a notion like *fanā'* (extinction of the individual soul) in different traditions does not mean they are de facto equal or that they lead to the realization of *fanā'* in the same way. Herein lies a grand trick of the devil! Beware of it, o disciple! The similarity in discourse or the meanings of the discourse can lead us to neglect what is alive in favor of what is dead. For instance, one might neglect a Prophet named Muhammad ﷺ who is right beside us, preferring Jesus ﷺ even though the former would be alive while the latter is not. This is a trap into which many have fallen throughout all eras, including within this final community, the community of the Last of all the Prophets ﷺ.

If indeed we find the flavor of the Gospel (*injīl*) in the Quran, it does not imply that the Quran and the Gospel are the same! While their source is singular—Allah ﷻ revealed all the Books—following the Gospel is not equal to following the Quran. Even without considering the alterations (*taḥrīf*) introduced to the ancient texts, and even if the Gospel or any other revealed Book were intact and preserved, it is no longer permissible to follow them, even if they contained only Truth from the Real. Two reasons account for this: the spiritual permission (*idhn*) and the epoch (*zamān*).

The time of the Quran has come; it is impermissible to follow another Book revealed by God while neglecting the Quran. As for the spiritual permission, it is embedded in the Quran. By its recitation, 10 "good deeds" are inscribed for each letter articulated by the reader. Therefore, reading the Quran equates to spiritual elevation, reward, and is undeniably beloved by God. As for reading other Books, it was prohibited by the Seal of the messengers ﷺ. We know from a narration that Sayyiduna Umar ibn al-Khattāb ؓ approached the Prophet ﷺ with religious writings from the Jews. This action angered the Messenger of God ﷺ, who then clearly elucidated the reasons for this prohibition: "I swear by He who holds my soul in His Hand that I have brought you a pure and clear message. Do not ask the people of the Book anything [about your religion] for fear they might relay a truth you could reject, or that they might share falsehoods you might accept. I swear by He who holds my soul in His Hand, if Mūsa were alive today, he would have no choice but to follow me."

However, some esteemed masters have paved the way by reinforcing the texts of our religion with those of previously revealed religions. They have demonstrated the breadth of this approach while respecting the boundary established by the Prophet ﷺ. For, if a biblical verse corroborates a Quranic verse, an authentic hadith, or a truthful statement from a master, then the information imparted by this biblical verse holds true. Similarly, the Quran and numerous hadiths inform us of the sayings and actions of the Prophets from prior communities. This adds value to the interpretation of our religion, especially on a spiritual level, without leading to misguidance.

Nevertheless, one constant must remain: commitment to the most recent truth over the older ones, for aligning with the present brings us in harmony with timeless truths. Conversely, clinging only to ancient truths detaches us from the core of reality. Within the Muslim community, established for over 14 centuries, we see many practitioners devoted to the pious predecessors (*salaf ṣāliḥ*), truly the best generation. But we often observe that these same people overlook subsequent righteous individuals and despise their contemporaries. This, too, is a trick of the devil! Without a genuine lineage connecting us to the predecessors (*salaf*), among whom the Prophet ﷺ is the best, mere knowledge of their lives and teachings cannot shield us from going astray. Just as mastering the Gospel didn't deter some Christians from disregarding Prophet Muhammad ﷺ in his era.

Assuming that guidance lies only in the past and is now unreachable due to a distant connection to the Prophet ﷺ is an error. Distinct Islamic sects have perpetually viewed each other as varying degrees of misguided based on their text interpretations. Without a living reference, mere attachment to a discourse doesn't ensure its embodiment in truth. Misguidance abounds even within guidance, just as guidance sends its luminous calls even amidst perdition.

A Major Pitfall of the Devil:
Know, disciple, that the notion that a particular spiritual "concept" from Sufi masters would correspond to a similar concept in Yoga, Taoism, or Buddhism, and therefore equate to the same thing, is profoundly mistaken. Even Heaven itself, despite being a tangible reward, can become forbidden to those to whom it was initially promised. Yet, they constantly speak of it, always believing they're moving towards it. What then of spiritual illumination? The fact that a great master may have theorized his own spiritual path through universal wisdom during his lifetime is acknowledged. However, adopting these wisdoms and applying them to one's own journey is an entirely different matter. It is evident that two speeches, identical in appearance, can be fundamentally contradictory, not in their form, but in their end goal. What misleads one and only superficially satiates his spiritual aspiration is for another, true sustenance that uplifts his soul and purifies his heart.

Without considering the variations in rituals that change from one religion to another, or even within different brotherhoods, what matters most is the ability to bridge the gap between substance and form. If prayer is merely a means to communicate with God and doesn't promote enlightenment, guidance, and the daily discernment of truth, then it ceases to be prayer. It becomes a litany recited out of habit and tradition. And this is the fate of every living path, transitioning from initiation to tradition. Ultimately, we engage in a series of rites without grasping their intended significance or outcome. Or, even if we do understand, we cannot attain them as those who came before us did.

Take, for example, two different sessions of Sufi dance (*ḥaḍra*). The first is carried out around a living master, who leads the dance.

Be assured that this session is alive, a meeting place for angels, a site of profound theophany for the Light of God and His Prophet ﷺ, and an assembly where various divine names appear, inspiring the followers. This is a true living space, between this world and the beyond, between heaven and earth, with people gathered around God's deputy.

Now consider another session of Sufi dance, performed without a living master, or with a "secondary" master whose role is merely to transmit earlier initiatic rites devoid of their essential lights. Here, we see people dancing, moving for God as they evoke Him. Is what they are doing permitted? Religious Law allows it. Is it commendable? It is counted as *dhikr*, thus commendable by the Law. But is there a genuine spiritual state, a secret, or a particular presence that will elevate the soul? No! The original intent is missed.

To an uninitiated observer, these two sessions might appear similar, and they might even prefer the lesser of the two due to a lack of discernment in their observation. But in truth, the two are polar opposites, even though both are within the permissible framework. However, a licit act disconnected from God becomes a grave deviation from the perspective of a spiritual journey, especially if this "separation from God" aspect escapes its participants. And this applies across all religions and paths. Everyone professes to address God, and in all traditions, some claim to perceive His responses. But not all stand equal, and not all are on the same stage of the journey.

Some are beckoned to move horizontally towards the truth, termed as *al-isrā'* (earthly journey), while others maintain a vertical relationship with God, referred to as *mi'rāj* (celestial ascension). For the people of *mi'rāj*, reverting to *isrā'* is a misstep. For those of *isrā'*, rejecting al-*mi'rāj* is an act of disbelief. The essence of *isrā'* is to advance towards the Truth, towards the "lower point" that will allow ascension to the "higher point." However, wandering aimlessly on a horizontal spiritual path, as most "seekers" do, isn't *isrā'* but spiritual tourism. And while worldly tourism is permissible, spiritual tourism represents a loss for the individual, the life that God granted them, and the destiny of the soul in the hereafter.

False Horizontality and True Verticality:
The doctrine of horizontality severs true verticality. This tendency to ideologically equate all different doc-

trines or spiritualities, without seeking the one that truly works for one at their time and place, is a devil's trap. It's a potent weapon for him, enabling him to mislead well-meaning souls seeking guidance. Even when most people no longer care, with this devilish stratagem, those who strive for success find themselves cut off from their goal due to deceptively positive and benign ideologies.

The truth eradicates horizontality, recognizing only a "lower point" for a "higher point." In other words, it recognizes only one deputy, one vicegerant (*khalīfa*) for a single God. And those who are not, are not on a horizontal line relative to the deputy, even if their speech appears similar in form. Instead, they are the dark side, the shadow of the truth. They are worse than overt misguidance! Overt misguidance, which glorifies reckless profit, excess, sexual freedom, individual self-determination, and the erasure of God from people's lives and choices... all of this is easily identifiable and doesn't claim to be on the same plane as the earth's deputy.

It's the false pretenders to God who are the real *tāghut*, those who lead people from Light to darkness while speaking to them of Light. It's a masterstroke of the devil: to make you glimpse a reality while distancing you as far as possible from it. His technique? We change definitions, we alter the steps leading to this reality. Instead of providing the shortest path, we guide you to contradictions that distance you. We horizontalize your relationship with God by making you seek similarities in all human "false sciences" and dead spiritualities. Then, you acquire an incredible technical vocabulary. Your intellect makes analogies of spiritual experiences in different traditions, and you believe you have understood the truth, while you have only distanced yourself from it, because we never grasp the truth. It is the truth that grasps us and leaves us dumbfounded.

The Role of the Vicegerent (*al-khalīfa*):

Compared to those who claim to possess spiritual paths leading to God, the vicegerent resets the clocks in his era. This is what `Īssa ﷵ, the son of Marriam ﵵ, did. He stood firm against the temple "merchants," who were only guardians of their own interests, because the true temple at that time was `Īssa ﷵ himself, and its guardian was none other than Allah ﷻ. He fulfilled his role on his own and watched over their true interests by calling them to the truth. He then said, "I was only sent to the lost sheep of the house of Israel."[61] Blessed are those who followed him. He was very clear about who he was, what his role was, and what he expected of those to whom he presented himself. The gospels contain words such as: "The time is fulfilled, and the Kingdom of God is near. Repent and believe in the Gospel,"[62] and also: "I am the Light of the world; whoever follows me will not walk in darkness, but will have the Light of life,"[63] and: "Whoever believes in me does not believe in me, but in the one who sent me—whoever sees me, sees the one who sent me."[64]

....

61   Matthew 15:24.
62   Mark 1:15.
63   John 8:12.
64   John 12:44-45.

The Prophet Muhammad ﷺ did the same, not only with his people or with the Christians but with all the worlds. All the religions known today were already present during his lifetime. And he distinguished himself from this group, which gradually became corrupt, to reveal the Truth. An authentic hadith illustrates this. In this hadith, the Prophet ﷺ says: "The one who believed in `Īssa and believes in me afterward will receive a double reward." In other words, the one who found what was closest to the truth in my absence and who found the truth with me will be doubly rewarded because he hit the mark twice. With this simple statement, he recalls the truth that was there before him and the one that must persist with him. As for the People of the Book who kept their religion, they weren't said to have a reward! On the contrary, their refusal of the truth in its new, more current form, that is closer to their time and location, is what will cancel their reward and their possibility of spiritual elevation. The vicegerent of the time emphasizes the importance of following him without hesitation. His message must be clear, and means provided for its spread. For all those it reaches, it becomes mandatory to annihilate all the false "verticalities" claiming to lead to God and to align oneself under the spiritual direction of the vicar of God on earth, the Saint of the Muhammadan community claiming such a role among Men. As with all his predecessors, he can only be a contemporary with clear discourse and evident proof.

41.
Interpretation of *Sūra* Al-Ḥujurāt

O disciples, today we delve into the depths of *Sūra* Al-Ḥujurāt (The Rooms). Ponder these words, for they reflect the insights and wisdom I wish to impart to you.

Allah ﷾ says in the Holy Quran: **"O you who have believed! Do not advance before Allah and His Messenger. And fear Allah. Allah is all-Hearing and Knowing."**[65]

This *Sūra* directly addresses those who have achieved the station of faith (*īmān*). Note the use of "*āmanū*," a term that distinctively addresses believers, not "O Muslims!" Allah ﷾ warns believers not to advance before Him and His Messenger ﷺ, urging them not to surpass the bounds set by the *sharī`a*. Understand this: a true Sufi respects the literal interpretation of sacred texts without layering additional interpretations upon them.

Yet, exoteric scholars often turn to interpretation. A fitting example is the interpretation of verse 115 of *Sūra* Al-Baqara (The Cow): **"To Allah belongs the East and the West. Wherever you turn, there is the Face of Allah. Indeed, Allah is all-Encompassing and Knowing."**[66]

....

65 Sūra 49. Al-Hujurāt, verse 1.
66 Sūra 2. Al-Baqara, verse 115.

Although we suggest it pertains to the essence, many self-proclaimed "literalist" scholars, through interpretation, deduce that He—exalted is He—envelops us with His Knowledge.

To shed more light, I shall discuss the three types of Sunna:

- The Sunna of speech
- The Sunna of action
- The Sunna of non-prohibition.

The Sunna of non-prohibition manifests as a mercy. A hadith shares an instance where the mother of believers, Aisha ﷽, enjoyed the Ethiopians' singing and dancing during a holiday, a performance which unfolded in front of the Prophet ﷺ without any objection. The Prophet ﷺ inquired, "What are they saying?" and was informed: "They sing, saying: 'Muhammad is a pious servant.'" He allowed the event to proceed, demonstrating his non-prohibition.

A Muslim should strive to enact the Sunna, regardless of whether it is comprehensible to him. Allah ﷻ indeed says: **"O you who have believed! Do not raise your voices above the voice of the Prophet ﷺ, and do not be loud to him in speech like the loudness of some of you to others, lest your deeds become worthless while you perceive not."**[67]

It's also crucial to discern whether a directive originates from the Prophet or the Messenger ﷺ. What does this mean? Let's explore. When it's from the Messenger, it relates to divine laws and thus the Quran. Had it meant

....

67   Sūra 49. Al-Hujurāt, verse 2.

not elevating our voice above the Messenger, it would suggest not exceeding the Quran and its teachings. However, this verse underscores the status of the Prophet ﷺ.

The Prophet ﷺ is invoked as a reminder, upholding the preceding law introduced by a Messenger or his own if he himself is a Messenger. "Nabī" (Prophet ﷺ in Arabic) derives from the term "*naba*," denoting not only "news" but also embodies the concept of reminder. This reminder is anchored in the *risāla* (Message). Thus, one should not elevate their voice above the Prophet ﷺ and should implement the Sunna without deviation. The beard serves as a tangible example of Sunna that some neglect, supplanting it with their customs.

Scholars have organized the Sunna by significance, prioritizing the action, followed by speech, and finally, non-prohibition. Interestingly, among the people of Allah ﷻ (*ahlullah*), the Sunna of speech precedes the others. This order can be justified as not all actions of the Prophet ﷺ are replicable by men. For instance, he married more than four women and fasted for seven consecutive days without eating nor drinking. Thus, some elements of the Sunna of action are unique to the Prophet ﷺ. As for the Sunna of non-prohibition, it symbolizes mercy. For example, despite the companions' initial desire to punish a Bedouin for urinating in the mosque, the Prophet ﷺ opposed their intent, suggesting they merely pour water over it instead.

In summary, the verse's interpretation emphasizes that when reading the Quran or when hearing "The Messenger of Allah ﷺ has said," one should remain silent, avoid raising their voice, and not be distracted, like by a phone, for example. Failing to adhere to this would imply raising one's voice above the Messenger's ﷺ.

"Those who lower their voices in the presence of Allah's Messenger are the ones whose hearts Allah has tested for piety. For them is forgiveness and a great reward."[68]

The pious, rewarded with forgiveness and vast rewards, refrain from raising their voices above the Messenger's ﷺ. Those who performed *dhikr* loudly received the Light of the Prophet ﷺ and subsequently performed *dhikr* in a subdued voice, so focused on their inner selves they couldn't hear themselves. This exemplifies Allah's ﷻ saying: **"the ones whose hearts Allah has tested for piety."**

"Indeed, those who call you from behind the chambers, most of them lack reason."[69]

Out of respect, we should address the Messenger of Allah ﷺ only when he is visible. The companions, may Allah ﷻ be pleased with them, frequently passed by the Prophet's ﷺ chambers and spoke only when he was in sight, refraining otherwise. The veiled message of this verse targets those who proclaim "O Messenger of Allah ﷺ" or "O Prophet ﷺ, I love you" without laying eyes on him. These individuals are the ones calling from behind the chambers.

....

68 Sūra 49. Al-Ḥujurāt, verse 3.
69 Sūra 49. Al-Ḥujurāt, verse 4.

"And had they been patient until you came out to them, it would have certainly been better for them. But Allah is Most Forgiving and Very Merciful."[70]

As mentioned, the companions patiently waited to see the Prophet ﷺ before addressing him. The underlying meaning of this verse alludes to disciples waiting for the Light of the Prophet ﷺ to illuminate their hearts before invoking him and sending prayers (*ṣalāwāt*) in his name.

....

70 Sūra 49. Al-Ḥujurāt, verse 5.

42.
An Era of Ignorance!

The current state of affairs reveals a striking truth: the essence, the heart of religion and the weight of deeds are founded on spiritual witnessing (*mushāhada*), not merely blind imitation or conforming to societal norms. It's not about, "I saw someone performing an act, so I will mirror it." No! When you engage in worship of Allah ﷻ, it should be rooted in unwavering certainty (*yaqīn*). Peace and tranquility should be the fruits of your worship. But remember, these feelings can only be begotten from a divine sign (*ishāra*) from the Lord. If you perform outward rituals without comprehending their inner spirit, if you approach religion without grasping its core essence, then you embody a hollow form of Islam.

Sadly, this is the pitfall into which many Muslims have descended, resulting in a landscape where one Muslim harbors hatred, envy, and even initiates conflict against another. We observe two armies clashing, one crying "*Allahu Akbar*," the other echoing "*bismillahi ar-Rahmāni ar-Rahīm*," as they engage in a fratricidal feud, each under the illusion of preserving the faith. But what faith does this reflect? There was once a singular religion, now bifurcated into two, as if serving two distinct gods.

When they encounter individuals proclaiming the existence of a Portal, a door, a conduit for divine secrets and profound meanings, they react with indignation, branding them as polytheists. What brand of polytheism are they accusing them of? Who are the real polytheists: those advocating for a single religion, in opposition to others who champion another, warring on the same battlefield over two versions of a religion that are, in essence, one, or those guiding souls to unlock the door of their hearts, to witness the Prophet ﷺ and His Light?

All glory to Allah ﷻ! This is a manifestation of profound ignorance. We are presently engulfed in an era eclipsed by a depth of ignorance unparalleled in history. Be not fooled by television and social media; they are not the bearers of genuine knowledge. True wisdom is steeped in the Science of Divine Names: **"and He taught Adam all the names."**[71] Your invention of a machine doesn't confer wisdom upon you. This machine will not aid your journey in the hereafter; it might even propel your descent into the Fire of Hell if employed unwisely.

....

71 Sūra 2. Al-Baqarah, verse 31.

43.
Are Your Fear and Sadness Justified?

To remain unafraid when others are fearful, or unsaddened when others are sad, one must first discern where genuine and valid fear and sadness lie.

Once you grasp the essence of real happiness, the tribulations that afflict others will no longer divert your attention. Instead, your sole focus will be on seeking the pleasure and approval of the Lord.

The Messenger of Allah ﷺ once remarked, "Indeed, among the servants of Allah ﷻ, there are those who, although not prophets, are envied by both prophets and martyrs." The companions inquired, "Who are these individuals, so that we may hold them dear?"

He responded, "They are those who, driven by the light of Allah's ﷻ love, hold deep affection for one another despite the absence of familial or blood ties. They radiate with luminosity, seated upon thrones of light. They remain fearless when others are struck by fear and are undisturbed by sorrow when others weep."

He then recited, **"Verily, for the friends of Allah (*awliyā' allah*) no fear shall come upon them nor shall they grieve."**[72]

....

72 Sūra 10. Yūnus, verse 62.

Excerpt from the Biography of
Shaykh Mohamed Faouzi al-Karkari

The following excerpt is from the biography of Sidi Shaykh Mohamed Faouzi al-Karkari, titled "At the Service of Destiny". This biography, authored by his disciple Jamal Zaghdoudi, has been translated into English by Professor Casewit. The passage provides a glimpse into the life and spiritual journey of Shaykh al-Karkari, quddisa sirruh. My intention in including this excerpt is to spark curiosity in those unfamiliar with the Shaykh and to inspire a desire to know more about him through this detailed and enlightening biography.

He is the sun of knowledge, the meeting of the two seas, the ocean of gnosis, the inmost heart of the spirit, the red sulphur, the inheritor of the secret of the essence, and the guide upon the Path of unveiling. He is the spiritual trainer, Shaykh Abu Abd Allah, Sidi Mohamed Faouzi b. Tayyib al-Karkari—may God sanctify his secret—of noble Prophetic descent, through Idrisi and Hasani lineage.

[...]

He is the son of the noble Sharif, Sidi Mūlay Tayyib al-Karkari al-Idrisi al-Hasani, son of the teacher, the shaykh, the Pole of his time, and the inheritor of the initiatic secret, Sidi Mūlay al-Tahir al-Karkari, may God sanctify his secret, son of Mūlay Muhammad al-Fardiy, son of Mūlay Tayyib, son of the shaykh and Pole Sidi Muhammad b. Qaddur al-Bukili, son of Mūlay `abd al-Qadir, son of Mūlay Ahmad, son of Mūlay al-`Arbi, son of Mūlay Muhammad, son of Mūlay Ali, son of Mūlay Musa, son of Mūlay Ali, son of Mūlay Yaaqub, son of Mūlay Ibrahim, son of Mūlay b. Zayd, son of Mūlay Yahya, son of Mūlay `Abd al-Rahman, son of Mūlay`abd Allah, son of Mūlay `Abd Al-`Aziz, son of Mūlay Zakariyya, son of Mūlay Yahya, son of Mūlay al-Hasan, son of Mūlay Muhammad, son of Mūlay `Ali, son of Mūlay `Isa, son of Mūlay Maymun Abu Wakili, son of Mūlay Mas`ud, son of Mūlay `Isa, son of Mūlay Musa, son of Mūlay `Azzuz, son of Mūlay `abd al-`Aziz, son of Mūlay Maazuz, son of Mūlay `Allal, son of Mūlay Jabir, son of Mūlay `Imran, son of Mūlay Salim, son Mūlay `Iyyad, son of Mūlay Ahmad, son of Mūlay Muhammad, son Mūlay al-Qasim, son of Mūlay Idris al-Azhar, son of Mūlay Idris al-Nafs al-Zakiyya, son of Mūlay `Abd Allah al-Kamil, son of Mūlay Hasan al-Thani, son of Mūlay Hasan al-Sibt, son of Sayyiduna `Ali—may God ennoble his face—and of Fatima al-Zahraa, daughter of the Master of the two worlds, Sayyiduna Muhammad ﷺ.

On his mother's side, he is the son of *lalla* Yamna who was the paternal cousin of Mūlay Tayyib, and the grand-daughter of Mūlay Muhammad al-Fardiy, and a niece of Mūlay Tahir, may God sanctify his secret. A shrine with a dome has been erected for each of his ancestors in the precincts of the town of al-Aroui. Many of them, besides being scholars of the Law, were granted the direct knowledge of God, which made them realized knowers through God. Thus, I have heard Sayyidi Shaykh Mohamed Faouzi al-Karkari say, "this blessing (*baraka*) has been transmitted from father to son over many generations."

His family has settled for twelve generations in [the surroundings of the town] of Al-Aroui, located in the Rif region of northern Morocco, twenty kilometers from the city of Nador.

[...]

Aged nineteen, Shaykh Mohamed Faouzi al-Karkari's spiritual state became so intense that he was isolated from his family and friends, and undertook a trip across Morocco for ten years. He visited several cities, reached distant places on foot, and walked among mountains and valleys. He went to Nador accompanied by Sharif b. al-Siniy, and spent what was left of his money for the ticket to the farthest destination he could afford; the city of Taza, where his boarding school was located. Then he continued his trip to Fes.

"The first night that we spent outside was on a road leading to the city of Sefrou, and the first city in which we stayed was Fes, close to the gate of Boujloud (*bab bujlūd*), a few meters from the taxi station... We did not know anyone, but after some time I recognized the different quarters of Fes, Mont-Fleuri, Zouagha... I remember a mosque where we spent many nights. After Fes, we travelled on foot all the way to Oujda where we stayed for three months. Then we went to Nador for three days, and finally to al-Hoceima where we spent a week. After al-Hoceima we walked all the way to Oued Laou. We would sleep under trees, and whenever hunger seized us, we ate leaves. Following Oued Laou, we continued our trip towards Tétouan, then Tanger, and we returned to Fes again.

From Fes we headed for Marrakech where we only spent two days, and we continued our trip towards Chichaouga, Agadir, Ouarzazate, Tiznit, Tafraout, Houara, until we reached Mahbes, during the first year of the militarization. We went back to Agadir and continued on to Rabat, in the suburb of Temara, where we stayed for quite a while, followed by Kenitra. I am only mentioning the cities, and not the towns and villages, such as Qacem, Marmousha, al-Hajeb, Ifran, Ain Rahma, Mūlay Ya'qub, 'ayn Shadya...

A year had passed since our initial departure. The second year, we started the Dour, visiting one moussem (religious festival) after another for forty-four saints buried within Moroccan territories. We slept in shrines and tombs of saints, such as Sidi Mūlay `Abdullah Amghar, where we stopped for a good while. We visited the moussem of shaykh al-Kamel, the commemoration (moussem) of Sidi `Ali b. Ḥamdush, Sidi Idris al-Azhar, and Mūlay Idris al-Akbar. Sometimes we would make thirty rounds between two tombs. In some cities, we spent a whole year, in others seven months, and in others only a few days. Hence, when a disciple tells us today that he comes from such and such city, we know who he is, because we have learned the characteristics of the inhabitants of that city during our pious roaming (*siyāḥa*), whether they are stingy or generous, gentle or rough..."

Shaykh Mohamed Faouzi al-Karkari—may God sanctify his secret—sometimes spent days and entire months alone crossing fields and mountains, sleeping wherever nighttime would seize him. "I took the earth as my bed, and the starry sky as my blanket. I travelled across the mountains but I entrusted my luggage with God... I was serving destiny without knowing it. Whenever I would supplicate God, He would respond to my supplication. Whatever I sought I obtained. Wherever I went, God's creatures turned towards me," he says.

While the days of hunger went on, our Shaykh would eat from garbage containers. In that state, he would hear trees and rocks speak to him and converse with him. He recalls, "We had isolated ourselves from people, and this made us talk to trees and rocks. We cannot keep count of all the saintly miracles that we experienced during those years of wandering."

"We lived with people whom you cannot imagine. We lived with the most degraded and humiliated people that exist, and yet we saw ourselves as more degraded than them because we believed that whatever they did would never equal the evil we had committed. We tried to take our lives, and God says that whoever slays a soul...it is as though he slew all of mankind. This is the reason why when someone comes to us now, no matter what his past is, he leaves us having turned to God in repentance. You may well preach to him (*da`wa*) all your life, but you will never affect him. Why? Because you have not experienced these states. You cannot guide or instruct someone if you have not walked the same road. Among those whom you call sinners, evil men, drunkards, and prostitutes we have encountered the most elevated men and women (`*illiyīn*), and we witnessed a hidden mercy in them. In some cases, these people become the best. When we became a Shaykh those whom we considered the most elevated proved to be the vilest (*suflī*), and this only added astonishment to our astonishment."

History of the Tariqa Karkariya

In addition to the biography of Sidi Shaykh Mohamed Faouzi al-Karkari, quddisa sirruh, I am including an inspiring excerpt about the early formative period of his tariqa from the same book, "At the Service of Destiny". Authored by Jamal Zaghdoudi and translated by Professor Casewit, this passage delves into the profound humility, spiritual elevation, and the unique path of succession that defined Shaykh Mohamed Faouzi al-Karkari's journey as a Sufi spiritual master. This snippet serves not only as an insight into the Shaykh's profound wisdom and spiritual excellence but also as a source of inspiration, illustrating the transformative power of true spiritual guidance and the deep connections within the Karkariyya spiritual lineage.

Given the excellence of his manners, as well as his mastery of the Path, Sayyidī Mohamed Faouzi received from Mūlay al-Hasan the permission (*idhn*) to transmit various invocations of the Path and to connect the wayfarers to the Path. However, he refused to transmit the litany (*wird*) while his shaykh was alive. Whenever someone asked him to join the Path, he directed him to Mūlay al-Hasan. This was due to his modesty and his love towards his shaykh.

When shaykh Mūlay al-Hasan passed away, our shaykh inherited the status of the shaykh of the Path despite the fact that this did not look obvious after Mūlay al-Hasan's death. Then he reached the highest stations and became a person towards whom all men and jinn seeking guidance were directed, without anyone knowing that he was a shaykh.

He says, "I attained to a level of nearness and knowledge after the death of my shaykh that he had not achieved himself during his lifetime." He continued in this way until the Real honored him with the station of Seal (*khatmiyya*), which is in reality the heritage of the divine names and of Muhammadan Successorship, (*al-khalīfa al-Muḥammadī*).

"The authorization to become spiritual master was made first by the shaykh, then by the Prophet ﷺ personally, and then by God. We never sought to become a shaykh, this fell upon us without us desiring it. It is a divine bestowal. The permission of this Path is from Ibn Mashīsh, for among all the Shaykhs of the initiatic chain, the only one to transmit the Light of allegiance as we do was shaykh Mūlay Abd al-Salam Ibn Mashīsh."

Sidi Mohamed Faouzi—may God sanctify his secret— spent a year alone, unknown by anyone, in complete obscurity (*khumūl*), so much that even his wife knew nothing about his state. She would see him wake up, make the ablutions, sit in the direction of the ka`ba (*qibla*), and perform invocation (*dhikr*) for hours. He was looking for someone to share the secrets of the Essence, for when the secret dwells in the heart the tongue cannot remain at rest.

The first disciples to join our shaykh were those who had followed Mūlay al-Hasan—may God be pleased with him—in his lifetime, namely our shaykh's mother, lalla Yamna, Sidi Abdel-Nasser al-Karkari, and Sidi Muḥammad b. Siniy.

Without a *zāwiya* and a gathering place, Sidi shaykh said, "The first course that we held was a commentary of shaykh Ahmad al-ʿAlawi's poems, followed by a commentary of Imam Ibn ʿAṭaʾ Allah al-Iskandari's aphorisms. During almost two years we explained the meanings of the aphorisms to the *fuqarāʾ*. We who did not understand any book became expositors of books... We gave such importance to those two books that after completing their commentary, shaykh Ahmad al-ʿAlawi and Imam Ibn ʿAṭaʾ Allāh al-Iskandari—may God be pleased with them—came to thank us in person in the spiritual realm (*malakūt*). Shaykh Ahmad al-ʿAlawi then enabled us to visit his *zāwiya* in Mostaghanem, and he showed us how he slaughtered a ram to inaugurate his *zāwiya*, which is why we slaughtered a ram too for the inauguration of our *zāwiya*."

The first twelve disciples who made the *khulwa* were: Sidi ʿAllal, Sidi Abdel-Nasser, Sidi Ahmed (Sidi shaykh's brother), Sidi Said Menouach, Sidi Muḥammad b. Siniy Taibi, Sidi Hajj Muhammad Fadhil, Sidi Abdel-Hafiz Ribaṭa, lalla Najat, Hajj Taieb Chérif alias al-Ouadi, Sidi Ahmad Boutaba, Sidi ʿAziz, and Sidi Abdel-Hamid. All of them experienced spiritual openings from which they benefited greatly. The Lights of the divine proximity and the brightness of supreme knowledge appeared to them. Sidi Shaykh says, "Our Path is one of vision in wakefulness, and whoever does not achieve vision I am not their shaykh and he is not my disciple." Thus, the Path began to take shape little by little until his fame crossed borders and oceans. Our shaykh continued to teach the secrets of the Name Allah in his *zāwiya* which is still located in al-Aroui.

Poems of the Shaykh

The following two poems by Shaykh Mohamed Faouzi al-Karkari have been translated into English by Professor Casewit. In presenting these translations, I have taken the liberty to make certain modifications where I saw fit, in an effort to preserve the essence and depth of the original Arabic text while making them accessible to an English-speaking audience. These changes were made with the utmost respect for the original meaning and spirit of Shaykh al-Karkari's profound words.

Poem 1: Beyond the Seven Gardens

Beyond the seven gardens
And the throne, and the pedestal
shone forth, the secret of Ihsan.

My sun was set ablaze,
the realms circled around me
I was taken from myself.

The All-Merciful gave me to drink,
From this cup drank I

Neither time, nor place
Neither speech, nor silence,
Neither angel, nor human,
Grasps the meaning of my kind.

I am the Kaf of Iḥsān,
I am the meaning of my holiness,
I am the sight of the blind,
I am the burier of the dead,
I am the door of goodpleasure
I am the spirit of intimacy.

I am the axial Pole among pillars,
For the Arabs, and the non-Arabs

I am the Judi of the age,
where Noah's Ark came to rest

On this day, and before
I am the wine within the jug,
In the realm of pure meaning,
and in the sensory realm.

Were that you knew, dear brethren,
The secret meaning of effacement!

I swear by the Criterion,
its ascending degrees of intimacy,
by the seven paired verses,
and by the Dome of holliness:

that the light of faith,
is a glimmer of my sun.

Poem 2: O God, I Seek Refuge in Thee from Thee
(Orison, munājāt, intimate prayer)

I seek refuge from proofs,
demonstrations, scales, and rulings

I seek refuge in Thee
from light that veils me from Thee

I seek refuge in Thee
from becoming a seeker or a fugitive

I seek refuge in Thee from being near or far

I seek refuge in Thee from descending or ascending

I seek refuge in Thee from invoking Thee

I seek refuge in Thee
from knowledge that serves as proof for Thee

I seek refuge in Thee from a resolve that causes
my soul to surpass others through its caprice

I seek refuge in Thee from a knowledge
that can be encroached upon

I seek refuge in Thee from a direct
knowledge (ma`rifa) that I take as an idol

I seek refuge in Thee from the sin of a direct
knowledge that would obliterate my ignorance

I seek refuge in Thee from a guise of organized
knowledge through which I would worship my caprice

I seek refuge in Thee from knowledge
of the herebelow and the hereafter

I seek refuge in Thee from letters
and the words that they form

I seek refuge in Thee from asking Thee

I seek refuge in Thee from not asking Thee

I seek refuge in Thee
from a lying heart and a truthful tongue

I seek refuge in Thee from asking for forgiveness
out of fear, or from supplicating out of need

I seek refuge in Thee from the affliction
of asking for an affliction to be lifted

I seek refuge in Thee from unveiling and veiling

Litany (*wird*) of the Tariqa

*This litany is traditionally performed twice daily: once
in the morning and once at night. It is important to be in
a state of ablution (wudu) before undertaking this practice.*

1.

*Bismillāhi ar-Raḥmāni ar-Raḥīm * alḥamdu lillāhi
rabbi-l-ʿālamīn * ar-rahmāni ar-raḥīm * maliki
yawmi-d-dīn * iyyāka naʿbudu wa iyyāka nastaʿīn *
ihdina-ṣ-ṣirāta-l-mustaqīm * ṣirāta-l-ladhīna anʿamta
ʿalaihim ghayril-maghḍūbi ʿalaihim wa laḍ-ḍāllīn (x7)
āmīn (x1)*

2.

*Bismillāhi ar-Raḥmāni ar-Raḥīm
wa mā tuqaddimū li ʿanfusikum min khayrin tajidūhu
ʿinda-allāhi huwa khayran wa ʿaʿẓama ʿajran
wa-staghfirū-llāha ʿinna allāha ghafūrun raḥīm*

*astaghfiru-llāha al-ʿadhīm ʿinna allāha ghafūrun
rahīm (x3)*

astaghfiru-llāh (x99)

astaghfiru-llāh ʿinna allāha ghafūrun raḥīm (x1)

3.

'inna-llāha wa malā'ikatahu yuṣallūna `alā-an-nabīy
yā 'ayyuhā-l-ladhīna 'āmanū ṣallū `alayhi
wa sallimū taslīmā

allāhumma ṣalli `alā sayyidina muḥammadin
`abdika wa rasūlika-n-nabiy-l-ummiyi wa `alā 'ālihi
wa ṣahbihi wa sallim (**x99**)

allāhumma ṣalli `alā sayyidina muḥammadin
`abdika wa rasūlika-n-nabiy-l-ummiyi wa `alā 'ālihi
wa ṣahbihi wa sallim taslīma (**x1**)

subḥāna rabbika rabbi-l-`izzati `ammā yaṣifūna,
wa salāmun `alā-l-mursalīna, wa-l-ḥamdu lillāhi
rabbi-l-`ālamīn

4.

shahida-llāhu 'annahu lā 'ilāha 'illā huwa
*wa-l-malā'ikatu wa 'ūlū-l-`ilmi qā'iman bil-qisṭ **
lā 'ilāha 'illā huwa al-`azīzu-l-ḥakīm * `
inna-d-dīna `inda-llāhi al-'islām

lā 'ilāha 'illa allāhu waḥdahu lā sharīka lah, lahu-l-
mulku wa lahu-l-ḥamdu wa huwa `alā kulli
shay'in qadīr (**x99**)

lā 'ilāha 'illa allāhu waḥdahu lā sharīka lah,
lahu-l-mulku wa lahu-l-ḥamdu wa huwa
`alā kulli shay'in shahīd (**x1**)

5.

*al-ḥamdu lillāhi al-ladhī hadānā lihadhā wa mā
kunnā linahtadiya lawlā ʿan hadānā llāh* *
laqad jāʾat rusulu rabbinā bil-ḥaqq

allāhumma laka-l-ḥamd **(x3)**
*(everything next preferably done while performing
prostration, sujūd, and facing qibla)*

al-ḥamdu li-llāhi wa shukru li-llāh **(x99)**

al-ḥamdu li-llāhi wa shukru li-llāhi kathīra **(x1)**

*subḥāna rabbika rabbi-l-ʿizzati ʿammā yaṣifūna,
wa salāmun ʿalā-l-mursalīna, wa-l-ḥamdu lillāhi
rabbi-l-ʿālamīn*

Quranic litany (highly recommended):

2 *ḥizb* (1 Juzz) per day

Sūra al-fatḥ, sūra ar-rahman,
sūra al-wāqiʿa, sūra al-ḥadīd
(preferably after the morning prayer)

Sūra ya-sīn and sūra al-mulk
(preferably after maghrib prayer).

BY THE SAME PUBLISHER

At the Service of Destiny

*A Biography of the Living Moroccan Sufi Master
Shaykh Mohamed Faouzi al-Karkari*

. . . .

In the Footsteps of Moses

*A Contemporary Sufi Commentary on the Story of
God's Confidant (kalīm Allāh) in the Qur'ān*

. . . .

Sufism Revived

*A Contemporary Treatise on Divine Light,
Prophecy and Sainthood*

. . . .

The Foundations
of the Karkariya Order

. . . .

Introduction
to Islamic Metaphysics

*A Contemporary Sufi Treatise on the Secrets
of the Divine Name*

. . . .

Wisdoms of the Heart

. . . .

The Sufi Path of Light

Printed and bound
in the United States of America

www.ingramcontent.com/pod-product-compliance
Lightning Source LLC
LaVergne TN
LVHW091702190726
843493LV00001B/115